Lecture Notes
in Business Information Processing　　　　472

LNBIP reports state-of-the-art results in areas related to business information systems and industrial application software development – timely, at a high level, and in both printed and electronic form.

The type of material published includes

- Proceedings (published in time for the respective event)
- Postproceedings (consisting of thoroughly revised and/or extended final papers)
- Other edited monographs (such as, for example, project reports or invited volumes)
- Tutorials (coherently integrated collections of lectures given at advanced courses, seminars, schools, etc.)
- Award-winning or exceptional theses

LNBIP is abstracted/indexed in DBLP, EI and Scopus. LNBIP volumes are also submitted for the inclusion in ISI Proceedings.

Daniel Mendez · Dietmar Winkler ·
Johannes Kross · Stefan Biffl ·
Johannes Bergsmann
Editors

Software Quality

Higher Software Quality through Zero Waste Development

15th International Conference, SWQD 2023
Munich, Germany, May 23–25, 2023
Proceedings

 Springer

Editors
Daniel Mendez ⓘ
Blekinge Institute of Technology
Karlskrona, Sweden

Johannes Kross
fortiss GmbH
Munich, Germany

Johannes Bergsmann
Software Quality Lab GmbH
Linz, Austria

Dietmar Winkler ⓘ
Austrian Center for Digital Production
(CDP), SBA Research gGmbH
Vienna, Austria

TU Wien
Vienna, Austria

Stefan Biffl ⓘ
TU Wien
Vienna, Austria

ISSN 1865-1348   ISSN 1865-1356 (electronic)
Lecture Notes in Business Information Processing
ISBN 978-3-031-31487-2   ISBN 978-3-031-31488-9 (eBook)
https://doi.org/10.1007/978-3-031-31488-9

This Springer imprint is published by the registered company Springer Nature Switzerland AG
The registered company address is: Gewerbestrasse 11, 6330 Cham, Switzerland

Message from the General Chair

The *Software Quality Days* (SWQD) conference and tools fair was first organized in 2009 and has since then grown to be the largest yearly conferences on software quality in Europe, with a strong and vibrant community. The program of the SWQD conference was designed to encompass a stimulating mixture of practice-oriented presentations, scientific presentations of new research topics, tutorials, and an exhibition area for tool vendors and other organizations in the area of software quality.

This professional symposium and conference offered a range of comprehensive and valuable opportunities for advanced professional training, new ideas, and networking with a series of keynote speeches, professional lectures, exhibits, and tutorials.

The SWQD conference welcomes anyone interested in software quality including: software process and quality managers, test managers, software testers, product managers, agile masters, project managers, software architects, software designers, requirements engineers, user interface designers, software developers, IT managers, release managers, development managers, application managers, and many more.

SWQD 2023 took place in Munich, May 23–25, 2023, and was organized by Software Quality Lab GmbH, Austria, TU Wien, Austria, Institute of Information Systems Engineering, Austria, and Blekinge Institute of Technology, Sweden. The guiding conference topic of SWQD 2023 was *"Higher Software Quality through Zero Waste Development"*, as changed product, process, and service requirements, e.g., distributed engineering projects, mobile applications, involvement of heterogeneous disciplines and stakeholders, extended application areas, and new technologies include new challenges and might require new and adapted methods and tools to support quality assurance activities early.

May 2023   Johannes Bergsmann

Message from the Scientific Program Chairs

The 15th *Software Quality Days* (SWQD) conference and tools fair brought together researchers and practitioners from business, industry, and academia working on quality assurance and quality management for software engineering and information technology. The SWQD conference is one of the largest software quality conferences in Europe.

Over the past years, we received a growing number of scientific contributions to the SWQD symposium. Starting back in 2012, the SWQD symposium included a dedicated scientific program published in scientific proceedings. In this fifteenth edition, we received an overall number of 10 high-quality submissions from researchers across Europe, which were each peer-reviewed in a single-blind process by 3 or more reviewers. Out of these submissions, we selected 4 contributions as full papers, yielding an acceptance rate of 40%. Further, we accepted 2 short papers representing promising research directions to spark discussions between researchers and practitioners on promising work in progress. This year, we have one scientific keynote speaker for the scientific program, who contributed an invited paper.

The main topics from academia and industry focused on Systems and Software Quality Management Methods, Improvements of Software Development Methods and Processes, Latest Trends and Emerging Topics in Software Quality, and Testing and Software Quality Assurance.

To support dissemination and collaboration with practitioners, scientific presentations were integrated into topic-oriented practical tracks. This book is structured according to topics following the guiding conference topic *"Higher Software Quality through Zero Waste Development"*:

- Social Aspects in Software Engineering
- Requirements Engineering
- Software Quality Assurance
- Software Testing
- Software Metrics
- Software Defect Prediction

May 2023

Daniel Mendez
Dietmar Winkler
Johannes Kross

Organization

Organizing Committee

General Chair

Johannes Bergsmann   Software Quality Lab GmbH, Austria

Scientific Program Co-chairs

Daniel Mendez   Blekinge Institute of Technology, Sweden
Dietmar Winkler   Austrian Center for Digital Production (CDP),
                                       SBA Research gGmbH, and TU Wien, Austria
Johannes Kross   fortiss GmbH, Germany

Proceedings Chair

Dietmar Winkler   Austrian Center for Digital Production (CDP),
                                       SBA Research gGmbH, and TU Wien, Austria

Organizing & Publicity Chair

Petra Bergsmann   Software Quality Lab GmbH, Austria

Program Committee

Matthias Book	University of Iceland, Iceland
Maya Daneva	University of Twente, The Netherlands
Oscar Dieste	Universidad Politécnica de Madrid, Spain
Frank Elberzhager	Fraunhofer IESE, Germany
Michael Felderer	German Aerospace Center, Germany
Gordon Fraser	University of Passau, Germany
Nauman Ghazi	Blekinge Institute of Technology, Sweden
Roman Haas	CQSE GmbH, Germany
Jens Heidrich	Fraunhofer IESE, Germany
Frank Houdek	Daimler AG, Germany

Marcos Kalinowski	Pontifical Catholic University of Rio de Janeiro, Brazil
Helena Holmstrom-Olsson	University of Malmö, Sweden
Marco Kurhmann	Reutlingen University, Germany
Eda Marchetti	ISTI-CNR, Italy
Kristof Meixner	TU Wien, Austria
Paula Monteiro	University of Minho, Portugal
Jürgen Münch	Reutlingen University, Germany
Oscar Pastor	Universitat Politècnica de València, Valencia, Spain
Dietmar Pfahl	University of Tartu, Estonia
Rick Rabiser	Johannes Kepler University Linz, Austria
Rudolf Ramler	Software Competence Center Hagenberg, Austria
Miroslaw Staron	University of Gothenburg, Sweden
Andreas Vogelsang	University of Cologne, Germany
Rini Van Solingen	Delft University of Technology, The Netherlands
Henning Femmer	FH Südwestfalen, Germany
Sebastian Voss	FH Aachen, Germany
Stefan Wagner	University of Stuttgart, Germany

Additional Reviewer

Lisa Sonnleitner

Contents

Social Aspects in Software Engineering

Conflicting Interests in the Hybrid Workplace: Five Perspectives
to Consider 3
  Darja Smite

Requirements Engineering

Requirements Quality vs. Process and Stakeholders' Well-Being: A Case
of a Nordic Bank 17
  Emil Lind, Javier Gonzalez-Huerta, and Emil Alégroth

Software Defect Prediction

Outlier Mining Techniques for Software Defect Prediction 41
  *Tim Cech, Daniel Atzberger, Willy Scheibel, Sanjay Misra,
  and Jürgen Döllner*

Software Testing

Applying a Genetic Algorithm for Test Suite Reduction in Industry 63
  Philipp Stadler, Reinhold Plösch, and Rudolf Ramler

Software Metrics

A Catalog of Source Code Metrics – A Tertiary Study 87
  Umar Iftikhar, Nauman Bin Ali, Jürgen Börstler, and Muhammad Usman

Software Quality Assurance

Software Quality Assessment: Defect Life Cycle, Software Defect Profile,
Its Types and Misalignments 109
  Oleksandr Gordieiev, Daria Gordieieva, and Austen Rainer

Comparing Anomaly Detection and Classification Algorithms: A Case
Study in Two Domains 121
Miroslaw Staron, Helena Odenstedt Hergés, Linda Block,
and Martin Sjödin

Author Index 137

Social Aspects in Software Engineering

Conflicting Interests in the Hybrid Workplace: Five Perspectives to Consider

Darja Smite[1,2]([✉]) [iD]

[1] Blekinge Institute of Technology, Karlskrona, Sweden
darja.smite@bth.se
[2] SINTEF Digital, Trondheim, Norway

Abstract. One clear legacy from the COVID-19 pandemic is the widespread adoption of remote work and flexible work arrangements, especially in tech companies. However, the practicability of remote working has raised a significant debate. The preferences for remote work vary greatly even among the employees of the same company. Individual wishes for remote vs office work can be often found anywhere on the spectrum from fully remote work to fully onsite with the hybrid working options of a varying degree in the middle. The most obvious common denominator in this situation is full flexibility, i.e., letting people decide when they want to work where. However, such one-fits-all strategy does not really fit anybody. Instead, it gives rise to several inherent conflicts of interest. In this position paper, we summarize opinions and experiences about remote work in five fictional personas as collective images based on extensive research: quantitative data, research interviews, and informal discussions with both employees and managers in tech companies, including Spotify, Ericsson, Telenor, Tieto, SONY, and many others. We conclude that increased flexibility at work leads to the conflict of individual interests of increased personal flexibility, team interest of efficient teamwork and corporate interests of preserving efficiency, company culture, and retaining the talents.

Keywords: Work-from-home · WFH · Remote work · Hybrid work · Managers

1 Introduction

The COVID-19 pandemic forced employees in tech companies (and beyond) worldwide to abruptly transition from full time work in the office to working entirely from home (WFH). Although WFH is not a new phenomenon (Pratt, 1984), the extent and the widespread adoption of remote work is unprecedented. Our observations two years later, after reopening of the societies, clearly suggest that many offices are half-empty (Smite et al., 2022a), employees request increased flexibility (Barrero et al., 2021a; Nguyen and Armoogum, 2021; Smite et al., 2023a) and new hires increasingly seek jobs that can be done remotely (Barrero et al., 2021a). In hindsight, the better-than-expected experiences with remote work during the pandemic seem to have forever changed the turn of the history in the magnitude of experience and perception of working from home

D. Mendez et al. (Eds.): SWQD 2023, LNBIP 472, pp. 3–13, 2023.
https://doi.org/10.1007/978-3-031-31488-9_1

(WFH) (Barrero et al., 2021a; Smite et al., 2023b). The dramatic shift in attitudes towards WFH over the pandemic swung from stigmatization of remote workers (Pratt, 1984) to increasing stigmatization of the slightest restrictions of remote working (Smite et al., 2023b). The latter are evidenced in an increasing readiness to resign and the rate of actual resignations (Barrero et al., 2021b) and the numerous publicly leaked or published letters of complains addressing corporate management that prohibits or limits WFH (e.g., the published exchange of letters at Apple[1]). Flexibility is desired by employees due to the perceived increase in productivity (often self-reported), job satisfaction, and well-being (Pratt, 1984; Russo et al. 2021; Smite et al., 2022a). Additional reasons for not willing to work in the office include unwillingness to commute, more comfortable conditions in the home office, convenience for running personal routines while at home, schedule full of online meetings, good weather conditions and the very habit of working from home (Smite et al., 2022a). So why would companies prohibit or limit remote work? The answer to this question is twofold.

On the one hand, it is a managerial issue. Remote work is associated with significant managerial challenges (Bailey and Kurland 2002). Managers repeatedly raise the question of whether "working-from-home" would not lead to "shirking from home" (Bloom et al., 2015). Many workers question and criticize the typical "Theory X style" management (McGregor, 1960) with a low perception of self-efficacy who do not trust the very ability of the employees to handle remote infrastructure, solve situations independently, manage time properly or work without supervision (Silva-C 2019). Such managers typically have a skeptical attitude towards remote work (Silva-C 2019). Despite increasing interest in agile ways of working and democratization of the workplace[2] (Olsson and Bosch, 2016), we must remember that corporate agility in large traditional corporations as well as in many regions with high power distance (even in tech industry) have not yet made a sufficient impact. Therefore, traditional management by direct supervision is admittedly still the most prefer management style. But even in modern companies with high levels of trust and autonomy granted to employees, managers repeatedly complain about the increased challenges of detecting and resolving conflicts when employees are completely or partially remote (Smite et al., 2023b).

On the other hand, the very notion of corporate culture is suddenly at stake. The "out of sight, out of mind" work mode has significantly increased the individualistic thinking and the "I over We" attitude. Researchers warn about the decreasing team efficiency (Miller et al. 2021; Tkalich et al., 2022), decreasing intensity of cross-company collaboration and the lack of new ties (Yang et al., 2021; Smite et al., 2023b), arguably decreased innovation capacity (Yang et al., 2021), and increasing risk of attrition due to deteriorating sense of belonging (Mortensen and Edmondson, 2023). The inherent conflict here is between the corporate interest in leveraging team efficiency, networked behavior, innovation and retention, and the individual interests in personal productivity and well-being.

---

[1] Apple employee letters to the Apple executive team signed by 3184 employees https://applet ogether.org/hotnews/thoughts-on-office-bound-work.html (Accessed on 2023-03-15).

[2] Democratization of the companies includes organizing less-hierarchically, larger autonomy given to the employees, great emphasis on employee empowerment, self-organization and self-management.

In this short position paper summarizing the keynote speech, we lay out five important perspectives on the practicability of WFH to consider. These are based on the extensive research: empirical data, as well as research interviews and informal discussions with both employees and managers in tech companies, including Spotify, Ericsson, Telenor, Tieto, SONY, and many others, and published research articles documenting the pandemic and post-pandemic experiences with WFH, remote and hybrid working in tech companies.

2   The Five Perspectives on Work from Home

Early studies of work from home show that remote work is not for everybody. While a large group of professionals feels more productive working from home and enjoys a better work-life balance, others report feeling unproductive, isolated, and burned out because of long work hours and the inability to separate work and private life when working from home (Russo et al., 2021; Smite et al., 2022b; Smite et al., 2023b). Evidently, employees with the opposite experiences will have completely different perspectives on the efficiency of remote work. The following figure maps preferences of employees from different companies on the spectrum of work arrangements (see Fig. 1). The portrayed picture shows the difficulty of modern management with no distinct country-specific peculiarities. The preferences seem to relate to corporate culture, but at the same time, they differ greatly within the same company too.

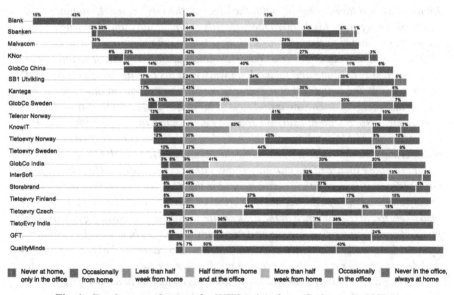

Fig. 1. Employee preferences for WFH (taken from (Smite et al., 2023a))

In the following, we describe five perspectives based on testimonies from practitioners (engineers and managers) who have been a part of our research since the pandemic.

The offered narratives portray fictional personas representing a collective image and featuring opinions, experiences, and aspects of character from multiple practitioners, thus not traceable to a single individual.

2.1 Remote and Hybrid Workers: A Flexibility is Every Employees Dream

The study of pioneers working from home or doing home telework published in 1984 starts with a futuristic vision of the white-collar labor force working in home offices (Pratt, 1984). Teleworkers of the past included "self-disciplined full-time clerical women seeking income at reduced personal expense, managerial and professional mothers wanting to nurture young children without dropping completely behind in their careers; and male managers or professionals who value the part-time integration of work and family life more than they do a competition for further advancement in their organizations" (Pratt, 1984). Three decades later, WFH is a norm across industries and countries and flexibility tops the list of most desirable benefits among the new hires (Barrero et al., 2021b). And while some companies still consider WFH as a conditional privilege, in the eyes of the employees it is more often than not viewed as their right.

Most proponents of the right to work from home are actually not considering working remotely fulltime but rather find themselves on a spectrum of hybrid work arrangements with a varying degree of remote work and work in the office (Smite et al., 2023b) (see also Fig. 1). In other words, the point for many is not to never leave home, but to be able to make autonomous decisions about where to conduct work duties.

John works in a large company with the office in the city center, 45 minutes of a train ride away from his home. One way. It's a Wednesday, the day when John normally commutes to the office to socialize, hold onsite meetings and work with others, as well as train in the gym. Yet, it is a sunny spring day, and it sounds more tempting to stay at home and take a long walk with his dog in the afternoon, and maybe even do the laundry that is still waiting for some attention after the hiking trip on the weekend. John yawns and says to himself: "Today, I will stay and work from home". No, no, do not suspect John of being selfish or sloppy with work. He is a very responsible employee. He knows what to do, he has more than ten years of experience in the current position in the company. He will also start working earlier (on the expense of the morning shower and commute time). He will connect via a videoconference with his teammates for the daily synch meeting with a cup of coffee and a bun, optimizing the time spent on having breakfast. In fact, John is also likely to eat a light lunch at the desk, while reading and answering emails. It's just that commuting on such a sunny day sounds like a very bad idea. Upon return from the long walk, John will check how much work is done and how much is left and decide whether a couple of evening work hours are necessary to compensate for the long walk. Or maybe he will invite Jane, his teammate and close neighbor to take a walk together and discuss the challenge she has faced recently. Previously, both of them have been onsite workers, but now they mostly meet for walks when working from home. Jane does not like commuting at all. The bottom line is – John is in control of his progress and schedule, and this flexibility feels great.

John is a typical example of the proponents of increased flexibility at work. Like Apple employees, he considers himself responsible and capable to work autonomously. Like many, he does not choose to work entirely remotely but prefers erratic presence in the sense that it is driven by his needs and wants rather than a predefined schedule.

2.2 Remote Employees: In Hybrid Teams We Are Second-Class Citizens

Individual freedom and flexibility come at a cost. The fact that one can make decisions about his or her workplace independently means that their colleagues can do the same. For some, decisions to work from home depend on good weather conditions and convenience for running personal routines at home, for many others it is about the unwillingness, inconvenience or length of commute, superior ability to focus in the absence of office noise and peer interruptions, more comfortable working, better coffee or food, or simply a matter of habit acquired during the pandemic forced WFH (Smite et al., 2022b). Unfortunately, the other side of the flexibility coin is the erratic office presence and inability to rely on collaborators being there when needed. While work in a fully remote or fully onsite team provides the level playing field experiences, work in hybrid teams is a different matter. In hybrid teams teammates alter days of work in the office with WFH days in an unplanned and unpredictable manner (Smite et al., 2023c) and thus experience reduced team cohesion, alienation of remoters and increased coordination difficulties (O'Leary and Mortensen, 2010; Santos and Ralph, 2022).

> *Jane works for the same company as John. They are both members of a hybrid team of eight engineers. During the pandemic, Jane moved from her tiny studio apartment to a larger apartment in the suburbs, where she has a home office with a garden view and a cat as a companion. It's much more comfortable to work from home, besides she hates trains. Jane is in the office for special occasions and large gatherings demanding everyone's presence. In contrast, some other colleagues are almost always onsite, four-five days per week. These are Jack (their team lead), Tanja and Bob. Fridays are the casual days when even these three may be remote. The most popular office days are Thursdays, when the local canteen serves pancakes. These are the days when Sonja and John are frequently onsite. Although Jane's team has worked together for a few years now, there is a feeling that remote work has resulted in a certain level of detachment. For her, there are fewer jokes exchanged with colleagues, no casual pair programming sessions and even the usual queries from Bob who is the most junior teammate are gone since she works remotely. In fact, there is another more junior teammate, Thomas, who has joined them during the last year. But Thomas lives in another town and works fully remotely, thus nobody has met him in person yet. Jane concludes that most of her challenges are probably because she is so rarely in the office, therefore, nothing to complain about. She still jokes with John when they arrange joint afternoon walks. Who knows, maybe the others, who are onsite also have the light humorous atmosphere they once had all together.*

Jane is a typical example of a remoter who works in a hybrid team and experiences what we call the feeling of being a "second class citizen" to the ones who are onsite.

Because Jane is a remoter, her onsite teammates do not reach out to her with questions, and she is unable to fully engage and follow what is going on, leading to the fear of missing out (FOMO) (Tkalich et al., 2022). It is possible that employees like Jane are likely to experience a more prominent decrease in job satisfaction than post-pandemic first hires because in contrast to the young generation of the employees they have experienced the more intense teamwork in the office from the pre-pandemic times but had to switch to working predominantly or entirely from home for one reason or the other.

2.3 Onsite Employees: Socialization is Essential for Social Wellbeing

Researchers distinguish between extraverts with high socialization needs and introverts with low socialization needs. Many thus assume that introverts are not very motivated to work in the office. Our observations, however, suggest that extraverts satisfy their socialization needs in various ways, be it in the office or outside of the work context, while introverts highly depend on the social connections at work.

> Bob is a young employee, who has joined the company shortly before the pandemic. He feels lucky to have managed to establish good relations with his colleagues before switching to the work from home mode because he is introverted and shy to reach out to people, he is not very familiar with. Remote work was very tough for him, especially because he is not very experienced. Working in isolation for Bob means that whenever he encounters a problem, he can get stuck for hours. In the office, Bob is more likely to ask for help and get unblocked. Similarly, during online meetings, Bob takes a passive role, while in an onsite meeting he is more likely to express his opinion or ask questions. Therefore, Bob celebrated the reopening of the offices when he could return to the fulltime office work. Unfortunately for Bob, not all of his teammates decided to return. But there are Jack (their team lead) and Tanja, who have both become his main mentors and friends. Then again, Sonja and John appear in the office every now and then, with a varying intensity. They would not have the same status of the go-to-persons for Bob, but he feels comfortable around them. Finally, he misses Jane, who used to be his mentor before the pandemic, but she has moved out of the city and pays very infrequent visits to the office. He feels their bond has deteriorated.

Bob represents the population of inexperienced employees who are introverted but is likely to demonstrate many typical behaviors of introverts in general. Employees like Bob form a vulnerable group of people whose work experience have changed dramatically with the rise of remote and hybrid work. Unlike the common belief, many companies report many introverts predominantly working in the office. The social ties and meaningful relations at work is what attracts them, not the superior comfort at work or any other practical motivation. And this is why, it is so important for the representatives from this group to meet others at work too.

2.4 Managers: Remote Work is a Managerial Nightmare

One of the main reasons why remote work was stigmatized and unexploited in the past relates to the managerial hurdles associated with employees working "behind a curtain"

(Bailey and Kurland 2002). Many remote work promoters have questioned the demands of office presence, criticizing the managers for the lack of trust in employees and the overreliance on direct supervision. But is this the main reason why managers want the employees back in the office?

Jack is a team lead of a team of eight engineers. Since the pandemic, his job underwent major transformations. First, everyone in the team was forced to work from home during the pandemic. A lot of Jack's time went into supporting the mental well-being of the employees and ensuring that everyone has the practical support needed to carry out their tasks from home. Although being significantly challenged to follow up with what is going on, Jack remembers the pandemic all remote period as a level-playing field experience, because everyone was online. With the reopening of the society and the offices, Jack's team members have expressed different preferences for organizing their work. Some work fully onsite, some choose to work hybrid and turn up every now and then, while others work predominantly remotely. Leading a team with such diverse preferences is not an easy task. Jack would not mind if everybody was remote or onsite, because it would provide similar work experiences among like-minded people. He personally likes working from home too. What Jack does not like is the inability to satisfy everybody's needs. For example, Bob and Tommy are relatively inexperienced and require support and mentoring from others, but Tommy is not in the office to observe his colleagues at work and receive a proper mentoring, while Bob has depended on the few colleagues who are in the office. Tanja, who is Bob's go-to person started to complain about the frequent interruptions. The burden of mentoring is evidently no longer equally distributed among the experienced members of the team. Further, when tensions in the team emerge, they are no longer visible to Jack. At least, when the tensions involve the remoters. In the past, Jack would spot when someone's body language or tone of voice changed and could follow up on what was going on. Detecting and resolving conflicts has become much more difficult in the hybrid work setup, as is the ability to provide satisfactory experiences for everyone during a hybrid meeting. Jack puts effort into moderating the hybrid meetings so that everybody has an opportunity to speak up, but similarly to the other onsiters he often gravitates towards those physically close in the room. To fight the feeling of detachment and sub-group formation, Jack considers requesting everyone to commute to the office at least a couple of days per week. But to be honest, Jack feels that his job satisfaction has dramatically decreased and considers pursuing the career as a consultant that he has once started.

It's reasonable to say that Jack is a representative of a rather typical team lead whose job tasks and the very nature of work has dramatically changed since the pandemic. Unlike the popular opinion that the promotion of office presence is Taylorism that belongs to the past, work in the office does provide the richest opportunities for managers to support the employees, as well as the employees to seek and receive support, from the managers and colleagues. We thus encourage to see the good intentions behind the manager's call for office presence. Satisfying everyone when their needs are anywhere on the onsite-hybrid-remote spectrum, and which furthermore may change at any given day, is truly an impossible task.

2.5   Managers: Remote Work is the Fall of Corporate Culture and Innovation

Finally, we conclude with the perspective of the managers responsible for the overall performance and atmosphere at work. Their work profile has also changed, similarly to team leads. However, the responsibility they carry is much higher. With the growing flexibility demands, they find themselves in front of an inherent conflict. Rooted in the strong believe that offices are not just walls but hubs that foster collaboration, community formation, sense of belonging, idea and information exchange, managers naturally tend to emphasize the importance of office presence. Some might even say that innovation is grounded in the spontaneous interactions at the coffee machines.

> *Michael, Jack's manager, is a head of the unit responsible for 22 engineering teams situated on two floors of the central office in the city, and a member of the corporate leadership group. Since the reopening of the offices, the employee well-being and office presence are discussed in the company leadership forum on a regular basis. One important reason for this is the growing number of resignations among the recent hires and the decrease in the sense of belonging scores in the bi-annual employee satisfaction survey. Michael and his leadership team has worked hard to find a strategy that would satisfy most of their employees. Concrete measures have been already taken to attract the employees back, including massive renovations and investments into mimicking the home coziness at the workplace by replacing cubicles with sofa areas for informal interaction, increasing the number of plants and art pieces, and even upgrading the coffee machines and local canteen offering with pancakes once a week, which seem to be very popular. Yet, the offices are mostly half-empty, and the managers are now considering forcing the office presence with two or three mandatory office days per week.*

Michael represents those managers who did not embrace the hybrid working (or "the new norm") and continue believing in the importance and value of the office interactions. These managers are not against the flexibility per se. After all, many tech companies had some flexibility even before the pandemic. However, they see no other means to guarantee efficiency, innovation, corporate loyalty and employee retention, other than through the office presence. Therefore, after a relaxed period of flexible working immediately following the pandemic, some companies introduce or consider introducing mandatory office presence, together with other attempts to lure the employees back into the offices (Smite et al., 2023a).

3   Concluding Remarks

The five perspectives on work from home described in this position paper illustrate the conflicting needs among the different employees and among the employees and the managers on different levels. In the following, we first summarize the different perspectives and then discuss the implications for practice to address the emerging challenges with the rise of WFH. A summary of the five perspectives emerging from our empirical studies are summarized in Table 1 together with the benefits and challenges of each of the emphasized interest groups.

Table 1. Summary of the Five Emerging Perspectives on Remote Work From Home.

Perspective	Office presence	Experiences with WFH
Employees working fully or partially remotely	Erratic office presence on the need and want basis	+ Increased flexibility + Control over own schedule + Avoidance of long commute + Time spent on commute
Remote employees working in hybrid teams	In the office for special occasions demanding presence only	+ More comfortable conditions + Time spent on commute − Fear of missing out (FOMO) − Lack of awareness about others − Feeling of detachment in the team
Introverted, shy and inexperienced employees working in hybrid teams	Predominantly in the office	− Reduced social circle, interactions primarily with onsiters, due to being shyness − Passive in online meetings
Team managers	Predominantly in the office	− Onsiters overloaded with queries − Mentoring efforts not evenly distributed inside the team − Decreased ability to detect and resolve tensions − Hard to moderate hybrid meeting in a way that provides equal experiences for remoters and onsiters − Decreased job satisfaction with the managerial role and duties
Company managers	Predominantly in the office	− Increased investments into office space renovations − Increased risk of resignation − Decreased sense of belonging among employees

Notably, the perspectives highlighted here are limited to the ones emerging from the empirical studies and by no means portray the complete picture. Other perspectives could be included, for example, of managers with positive attitudes, extraverted employees working onsite, employees working in fully remote teams, etc.

Evidently, the experiences summarized in Table 1 can be characterized as mixed from the individual perspective as there are both positive and negative aspects for different individual employees, and rather negative from the managerial perspective, confirming the view point that remote work is full of managerial issues (Bailey and Kurland, 2002). However, we also emphasize that this is primarily due to the hybrid work arrangement and inability to find a one-fits-all strategy for organizing the work in a team with diverse preferences. Future work thus needs to focus on better understanding the differences between managing hybrid and fully remote teams, as well as on exploring the benefits of increased remote work on the team and organizational level.

Acknowledgement. This research is funded by the Swedish Knowledge Foundation within the WorkFlex project (KK-Hög grant 2022/0047) and the S.E.R.T. research profile project (grant 2018/010).

References

Barrero, J.M., Bloom, N., Davis, S.J.: Why working from home will stick (no. w28731). National Bureau of Economic Research (2021a)

Barrero, J.M., Bloom, N., Davis, S.J.: Let me work from home, or i will find another job. University of Chicago, Becker Friedman Institute for Economics Working Paper, 2021-87 (2021b)

Bailey, D.E., Kurland, N.B.: A review of telework research: findings, new directions, and lessons for the study of modern work. J. Organ. Behav. Int. J. Ind. Occup. Organ. Psychol. Behav. **23**(4), 383–400 (2002)

Bloom, N., Liang, J., Roberts, J., Ying, Z.J.: Does working from home work? Evidence from a Chinese experiment. Q. J. Econ. **130**(1), 165–218 (2015)

McGregor, D.M.: The human side of enterprise. In: Readings in Managerial Psychology, pp. 310–321. The University of Chicago Press (1960)

Miller, C., Rodeghero, P., Storey, M.A., Ford, D., Zimmermann, T.: How was your weekend? Software development teams working from home during COVID-19. In: 2021 IEEE/ACM 43rd International Conference on Software Engineering (ICSE), pp. 624–636 (2021)

Mortensen, M., Edmondson, A.C.: Rethink Your Employee Value Proposition: Offer your people more than just flexibility. Harvard Bus. Rev. **101**(1–2), 45–49 (2023)

Nguyen, M.H., Armoogum, J.: Perception and preference for home-based telework in the Covid-19 era: a gender-based analysis in Hanoi, Vietnam. Sustainability **13**(6), 3179 (2021)

Olsson, H.H., Bosch, J.: No more bosses? In: Abrahamsson, P., Jedlitschka, A., Duc, A.N., Felderer, M., Amasaki, S., Mikkonen, T. (eds.) PROFES 2016. LNCS, vol. 10027, pp. 86–101. Springer, Cham (2016). https://doi.org/10.1007/978-3-319-49094-6_6

O'Leary, M.B., Mortensen, M.: Go (con) figure: subgroups, imbalance, and isolates in geographically dispersed teams. Organ. Sci. **21**(1), 115–131 (2010)

Pratt, J.H.: Home teleworking: a study of its pioneers. Technol. Forecast. Soc. Change **25**(1), 1–14 (1984)

Russo, D., Hanel, P.H.P., Altnickel, S., van Berkel, N.: Predictors of well-being and productivity among software professionals during the COVID-19 pandemic – a longitudinal study. Empir. Softw. Eng. **26**(4), 1–63 (2021). https://doi.org/10.1007/s10664-021-09945-9

de Souza Santos, R.E., Ralph, P.: Practices to improve teamwork in software development during the COVID-19 pandemic: an ethnographic study. In: Proceedings of the 15th International Conference on Cooperative and Human Aspects of Software Engineering, pp. 81–85 (2022)

Silva-C, A.: The attitude of managers toward telework, why is it so difficult to adopt it in organizations? Technol. Soc. **59**, 101133 (2019)

Smite, D., et al.: Half-empty offices in flexible work arrangements: why are employees not return-ing? In: Taibi, D., Kuhrmann, M., Mikkonen, T., Klünder, J., Abrahamsson, P. (eds.) Product-Focused Software Process Improvement. PROFES 2022 LNCS, vol. 13709, pp. 252–261. Springer, Cham (2022a). https://doi.org/10.1007/978-3-031-21388-5_18

Smite, D., Tkalich, A., Moe, N.B., Papatheocharous, E., Klotins, E., Buvik, M.P.: Changes in per-ceived productivity of software engineers during COVID-19 pandemic: the voice of evidence. J. Syst. Softw. **186**, 111197 (2022b)

Smite, D., Moe, N.B., Hildrum, J., Gonzalez Huerta, J., Mendez, D.: Work-from-home is here to stay: call for flexibility in post-pandemic work policies. J. Syst. Softw. **195**, 111552 (2023a)

Šmite, D., Moe, N.B., Klotins, E., Gonzalez-Huerta, J.: From forced working-from-home to voluntary working-from-anywhere: two revolutions in telework. J. Syst. Softw. **195**, 111509 (2023b)

Smite, D. Christensen, E.L., Tell, P., Russo, D.: The future workplace: characterizing the spectrum of hybrid work arrangements for software teams. IEEE Softw. **40**(2), 34–42 (2023c)

Tkalich, A., Šmite, D., Andersen, N.H., Moe, N.B.: What happens to psychological safety when going remote? IEEE Softw. (2022, in press)

Yang, L., et al.: The effects of remote work on collaboration among information workers. Nat. Hum. Behav. **6**(1), 43–54 (2021)

Requirements Engineering

Requirements Quality vs. Process and Stakeholders' Well-Being: A Case of a Nordic Bank

Emil Lind, Javier Gonzalez-Huerta$^{(\boxtimes)}$, and Emil Alégroth

Software Engineering Research Lab SERL, Blekinge Institute of Technology,
371 79 Karlskrona, Sweden
{emil.lind,javier.gonzalez.huerta,emil.alegroth}@bth.se

Abstract. Requirements are key artefacts to describe the intended purpose of a software system. The quality of requirements is crucial for deciding what to do next, impacting the development process' effectiveness and efficiency. However, we know very little about the connection between practitioners' perceptions regarding requirements quality and its impact on the process or the feelings of the professionals involved in the development process.

Objectives: This study investigates: i) How software development practitioners define requirements quality, ii) how the perceived quality of requirements impact process and stakeholders' well-being, and iii) what are the causes and potential solutions for poor-quality requirements.

Method: This study was performed as a descriptive interview study at a sub-organization of a Nordic bank that develops its own web and mobile apps. The data collection comprises interviews with 20 practitioners, including requirements engineers, developers, testers, and newly employed developers, with five interviewees from each group.

Results: The results show that different roles have different views on what makes a requirement good quality. Participants highlighted that, in general, they experience negative emotions, more work, and overhead communication when they work with requirements they perceive to be of poor quality. The practitioners also describe positive effects on their performance and positive feelings when they work with requirements that they perceive to be good.

Keywords: Requirements Engineering · Requirements Quality · Human Factors · Empirical Study

1 Introduction

Requirements are crucial for developing software-intensive products and services since they are the main link between the business value and its implementation. As such, the consequences of issues—Poor quality such as incompleteness or ambiguity—with requirements might lead to a project or product failure

D. Mendez et al. (Eds.): SWQD 2023, LNBIP 472, pp. 17–37, 2023.
https://doi.org/10.1007/978-3-031-31488-9_2

[12,16,17]. Requirements are used by multiple roles, including developers, testers, and user experience designers in their daily work [7]. Therefore, requirements quality has a profound, direct impact on the outcome of the different downstream activities in the development process and on the quality of the final product itself [7].

Moreover, changes to requirements have an intrinsic relationship to project failure and results in projects not being finished within time or budget constraints [21]. Changes to requirements, before and after release, affect the different development activities [9,11], for instance, by forcing the re-prioritization of tasks and effort allocation.

Several standards define how to write good requirements (e.g., ISO29148 [10] or IREB [2]) and have also been studied in several research works (e.g., [7,17]). These works aim to provide an objective, general view of how a good quality requirement should be, although there is still a lack of a holistic perspective on quality factors on requirements [9]. Moreover, from a practitioner's view, there is a lack of understanding regarding what they perceive as good - or bad- requirements and how they affect their daily work. Following Femmer's and Vogelsang's activity-based view on requirements and their quality [7], it is highly relevant to identify the practitioners' view on requirements quality and how practitioners subjectively define it. The reason is that standards are often too general or imprecise to be applied in different industries. Following this reasoning, eliciting developers', testers', and requirements engineers' experiences and how they are affected by what they perceive to be bad requirements - compared to what they perceive to be good requirements - is therefore of importance. The reason is that the practitioners' needs may not align with what is prioritized in the standards. Thus, research into the phenomenon provides insights into these practitioners' ways of working and inputs for future improvements to said requirements standards.

There are research works that analyze the impact of good/bad requirements on the project outcomes (e.g., [4,12,16–18]). However, these are either based on questionnaire surveys or directly based on static analysis techniques. Thereby leaving a gap in knowledge from empirical case studies that go deeper, through interviews and focus groups, to understand the consequences of good and bad quality requirements as the practitioners perceive them.

This study investigates the differences in how practitioners from different roles define good and bad requirements, i.e., what characteristics make requirements good quality. Additionally, the study aims to determine the impact practitioners experience from good or bad quality requirements in their work, workload, and well-being. Furthermore, the study also aims to find the perceived causes and potential solutions to poor quality requirements. The goal is also to gain an understanding of requirements quality, which is essential first to align with existing standards but also to understand what are good-enough requirements that allow organizations to prioritize requirements for implementation that add value to the product [5].

The remainder of the paper is structured as follows: Section 2 discusses related research in the area. Section 3 describes the research methodology followed in the interview study. Section 4 reports the main results of the study. Section 5 discusses the main findings. In Sect. 6 we discuss the limitations and threats to the validity. Finally, Sect. 7 draws the main conclusions and discusses further works.

2   Related Work

Requirements Engineering (RE) in general and specific RE methods are well represented in the body of scientific knowledge. There are also recommendations and guidelines for working with RE and even quality standards for requirements (e.g., [2,10]).

The NaPiRE [16,17] project, which involves more than 200 companies in 10 countries, has mapped several kinds of bad requirements with factors for project failure or linked these requirements problems with project delays or budget overruns. Similarly, several studies (e.g., [4,11,12,21]) have tried to find relationships between requirements quality to requirements (i.e., requirements smells [6]). However, what is still unclear is what the impact of these smells would be. Femmer and Vogelsang [7] found a relationship between the quality of requirements and the *quality in use* of the software system being developed. Frattini et al. [9] developed an ontology, scrutinizing 105 research primary studies, with the goal of providing a more harmonized view of requirements quality factors.

However, neither the NaPiRE project nor the studies mentioned above have considered the different perceptions of what good or bad requirements are for different roles or the effect that bad requirements might have on the practitioners' work, workload and well-being. Well-being, especially stress has been found as an important factor for hindering collaborative work and technical practices [15]. All these aspects are essential to define good-enough requirements that allow organizations to prioritize requirements for implementation that add value to the product [5], thus motivating their study in the area of RE.

3   Research Methodology

The study addressed the following research questions:

- **RQ1** How do software development practitioners define requirements quality?
- **RQ2** How does the perceived quality of requirements impact the work and wellbeing of practitioners in software development?
- **RQ3** What are the perceived causes and potential solutions of the poor quality of requirements?

The intent is to map the effects of low-quality requirements (as per RQ1), as perceived by requirements engineers, developers, and testers, to the enjoyment of

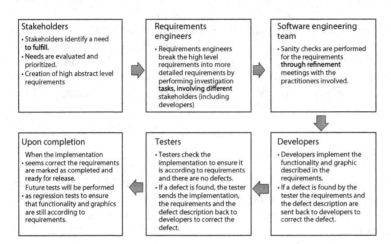

Fig. 1. Requirements Workflow

work, stress, and well-being in general, as the perception of their colleagues, organization, and workload. Hence, the results lean into the human factors domain of software engineering or behavioural software engineering [13]. Such results, albeit often less tangible than technical factors, are essential for the general understanding of software engineering.

3.1 Context, Case, and Unit of Analysis

To address the research questions mentioned above, we conducted an interview study in an industrial setting comprising twentyfive interviews with software development practitioners. We conducted the study in a sub-organization of a Nordic bank[1] which develops mobile and web apps for the bank's end-users, therefore belonging to the financial technology (fintech) domain.

The organization has development teams organized into different areas, such as product areas or business/domain areas, referred to as projects. On average, the development teams consist of 10 to 12 employees and contain roles such as requirements engineers, testers, developers, UX designers, and scrum masters. Note that the studied organization, although has incorporated many agile rituals and practices, carries out requirements engineering, development and software testing in a waterfall-like process, i.e., there is a hand-over between requirements engineers to developers and later from developers to testers. Figure 1 provides a visual, brief overview of the development workflow used at the organization.

In this study, we focus on four different *units of analysis*, i.e., requirements engineers, testers, software developers with more than one year of experience at the organization and recently recruited software developers. Employees from each group were selected, by a hybrid of convenience and random sampling [14],

---

[1] Fictitious name to preserve anonymity.

Table 1. Demographic information of the interview participants, including interviewee Id, participant's working location, and years of experience within the organisation

Interviewee Id (including role)	Location	Experience
Requirements Engineering 1	Sweden	<5 years
Requirements Engineering 2	Sweden	>5 years
Requirements Engineering 3	Baltic Country	>5 years
Requirements Engineering 4	Sweden	<5 years
Requirements Engineering 5	Sweden	>5 years
Developer 1	Sweden	<5 years
Developer 2	Sweden	<5 years
Developer 3	Sweden	>5 years
Developer 4	Sweden	<5 years
Developer 5	Sweden	<5 years
Tester 1	Sweden	>5 years
Tester 2	Baltic Country	<5 years
Tester 3	Baltic Country	<5 years
Tester 4	Sweden	<5 years
Tester 5	Baltic Country	<5 years
Recently recruited developer 1	Sweden	<3 months
Recently recruited developer 2	Sweden	<3 months
Recently recruited developer 3	Sweden	<3 months
Recently recruited developer 4	Sweden	<3 months
Recently recruited developer 5	Sweden	<3 months

from different projects and geographic locations to acquire a more representative sample inside the organization. The hybrid sampling consisted of using a list of employees with suitable characteristics for the study provided by managers at the organization. We refer to this as hybrid sampling since the authors had limited control over which participants were added to the list, i.e. the participants' managers ultimately were the ones suggesting their participation in the study. We selected the organization also by convenience since it is one of the partner companies in an ongoing research project that focuses, among other topics, on addressing the quality degradation of software assets. Table 1 details the participants' demographic information.

The recently recruited developers were an opportunity-based unit of analysis, interviewed to complement the results from the study's three central units of analysis (i.e., requirements engineers, testers, and developers). We sampled these participants following the same approach as the other participants. However, the sample frame of potential participants was much smaller, i.e. only employees with less than four months of employment were eligible. However, since we exercised no control over the selection, we still classify it as hybrid convenience and random selection.

In total, we conducted interviews with 20 participants; five requirements engineers, five developers, five testers, and five recently recruited developers. We interviewed the recently recruited developers twice, the first time when they had finished or were close to finishing their onboarding at the organization and the

second time when they had worked for a few more months at the organization[2]
Therefore the total number of interviews conducted in the study was 25.

To ensure anonymity, we clustered the participants' experience into groups
of more than five years, less than five years (the requirement for participating
was at least a year in the organization), and three months or less for the recently
recruited developers.

3.2 Data Collection

Data for this interview study was collected using semi-structured interviews. The
first part of the interview guide aimed at answering RQ1, whilst the second part
of the interview aimed at answering RQ2 and RQ3.

Each interview took thirty to sixty minutes, following a predefined interview
guide[3], recorded with audio and video, and later transcribed to text. The interview guide consisted of 16 predefined questions for the testers and developers
that had worked in the organization for at least one year. For requirements engineers, the interview guide consisted of 24 predefined questions, 19 predefined
questions for the first interview with the recently recruited developers and 15
predefined questions for the second interview with the recently recruited developers. Although the interview guides varied depending on the interviewees' roles,
the semantic information gathered aimed at providing complementing answers
to the research questions. The guides also had questions that are not mapped
to any specific research question. We added these additional questions to gather
supplementary information to understand the context and to interpret the interview results that contributed to the research questions. The number of predefined
questions was decided to give enough time to ask follow-up questions.

3.3 Data Analysis

The interviews were analyzed using thematic analysis [1,3]. Open coding was
used, where codes were generated based on the semantic meaning of statements
from the interview transcripts, using mainly a deductive approach [3]. We used
the coded information and the associated quotes to synthesize evidence from the
collected data. This evidence-driven analysis approach was suitable for answering
the research questions due to the study's descriptive nature.

We added the codes incrementally from the interview results. As stated, the
codes were formulated based on the semantic meaning of the interviewees' statements. When another statement was found to contain similar semantic information, said the statement was marked with the same code. We did not restrict

---

[2] Although the analysis of the differences between these two interview instances is out
of the scope of this paper.

[3] The interview guide is available in the companion materials in Zenodo DOI:
10.5281/zenodo.7306032.

coding to a 1-to-1 mapping between codes and statements. Hence, we could code a statement with one or several codes. We stored all extracted statements from the transcripts with the codes in the code books for consistency.

The rationale for using coding was to provide an overview of the data to connect statements and observations to draw higher-level conclusions. For example, the statement "Requirements are changed with time. We do not work in waterfall projects when a requirement is thought to be completed, cannot be changed, and then handed over to the developer. We have a parallel work in which we often realize that something was not expressed in a good way, it is often that we change the wording or more things a bit". was coded with the code "Changes during development". Similarly, the statement; "We mostly work with drafting the requirements during the sprint as they are not complete when we bring them into the sprint, so a part of our task is to make an investigation" were coded with the same code.

The coding resulted in synthesized themes organized in a document with related codes and key sentences. After the themes had been defined, they were used to draw conclusions on the appropriate level of abstraction to answer the research questions.

As thematic coding, with semantic equivalence partitioning, is subject to researcher bias, the first author validated the coding scheme with the second and third authors. We conducted this validation in the early stages of the analysis process. This was achieved by providing the second and third authors with an interview transcript and the codebook. The authors coded the corresponding transcript using the codebook. After the coding, the results were compared based on similarity. Results showed a high similarity: 74% of the codes matched. We calculated this percentage as the number of sentences tagged with the same codes divided by the total number of coded sentences. This result was considered sufficient for the first author to proceed with the rest of the coding.

4 Results

This section presents the results of the interview study. First, we summarize how requirements are handled and utilized in Nordic Bank, and the perceived prevalence of bad requirements. The results that aim at answering research questions RQ1, R2, and RQ3 are presented in Subsects. 4.2, 4.3, and 4.4, respectively.

4.1 Requirements Engineering Process at Nordic Bank

This subsection presents the results that the participants provided in regard to the ways Nordic Bank utilizes requirements during the development process. We also include a brief analysis of the prevalence of bad requirements in the organization.

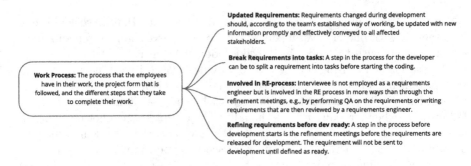

Fig. 2. Requirements work-process-related codes

Workprocess. Figure 2 presents the code book for the codes related to how requirements are handled during the development process. Four testers reported that they were involved in the requirements engineering process and performed requirements quality assurance activities. The developers also mentioned that within their teams, they carry out requirements refinement activities—Activities aimed at improving the content and understandability of the requirements—before the requirement reaches the status of *ready-to-develop*.

Participants mentioned that it is possible to update the requirements once the development has started, but in those cases, all stakeholders should be informed about the change. Finally, it was reported that it is a common practice to split requirements into smaller tasks to be carried out by the team or other teams.

Bad Requirements Prevalence. The testers involved in the quality assurance process for the requirements stated that the requirements, in general, in their understanding, were of good quality. Additionally, they stated that they write preliminary test cases for all requirements, including edge case tests. Despite these efforts, they still discover many defects when they test the implementation. One interviewee stated, "I think the quality is quite high, but that does not mean that if the requirements are good, the developers won't make mistakes and bugs [...] It would seem that we have bad user stories if I say that I give back 75% of the stories for fixing because I find bugs". The same tester thought that it was mostly the developers' own fault and not caused by bad requirements, "It is not that they don't understand or that might not mean that the requirements are bad, but this is just that they might not read the story enough or maybe interpret something differently".

A statement from a tester that did not perform QA checks on requirements before handing them to developers stated, "It's important that I as a tester and the developers both understand it [the requirement] as it is written" when describing good requirements. Another interviewee stated, regarding require-ments quality, "If you are new in an area and in your role, then there is a higher demand on the quality of the requirements". Another tester involved with the RE process experienced that defects, in one-third to half of the times, were caused

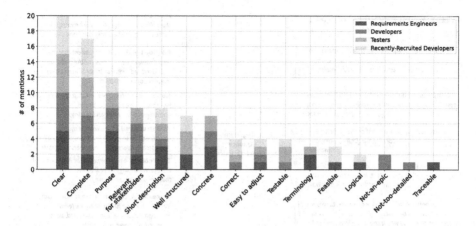

Fig. 3. Quality Characteristics of Good and Bad Requirements

by bad requirements "It's like 50–50. It doesn't need to be bad requirements; it might be that some developer has missed something. But maybe less than 50%, maybe 30% are bad requirements". However, because the actual requirements were not analyzed in the study, the testers' experiences are still unverified. The developers, testers, and requirements engineers agreed upon one point: refinement meetings are part of their RE-process. Still, they estimated the frequency of bad requirements to be about 10–25% of the requirements.

4.2 RQ1: How Software Development Practitioners Define Requirements Quality?

Figure 3 illustrates the requirements quality characteristics mentioned by the participants. The number of mentions accounts for each interviewee that mentioned each quality characteristic during the interviews.

Every interviewee mentioned *clear* as a characteristic of a good requirement. However, as clear might have multiple interpretations of what it means, which also can vary among roles, some interviewees might have mentioned this characteristic as a collective term for other characteristics, e.g., unambiguous and/or complete. Regardless, it seems that clarity, associated with ease of understanding, is considered a pivotal characteristic for all interviewees. A tester said when describing good characteristics of requirements that "Clarity is, as mentioned, a keyword here, and there can be several different aspects that can make it [a requirement] clear".

The characteristic *complete* was described by every developer, and most testers agreed that requirements have to be complete when they receive them. Some testers pointed out that changing a requirement while in testing would make the process much more complex. Only three requirements engineers explicitly mentioned complete as a characteristic of good requirements. However, one of those three requirements engineers pointed out that they accept, in their team,

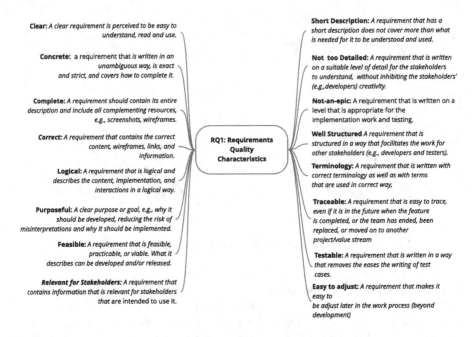

Clear: *A clear requirement is perceived to be easy to understand, read and use.*

Concrete: *a requirement that is written in an unambiguous way, is exact and strict, and covers how to complete it.*

Complete: *A requirement should contain its entire description and include all complementing resources, e.g., screenshots, wireframes.*

Correct: *A requirement that contains the correct content, wireframes, links, and information.*

Logical: *A requirement that is logical and describes the content, implementation, and interactions in a logical way.*

Purposeful: *A clear purpose or goal, e.g., why it should be developed, reducing the risk of misinterpretations and why it should be implemented.*

Feasible: *A requirement that is feasible, practicable, or viable. What it describes can be developed and/or released.*

Relevant for Stakeholders: *A requirement that contains information that is relevant for stakeholders that are intended to use it.*

RQ1: Requirements Quality Characteristics

Short Description: *A requirement that has a short description does not cover more than what is needed for it to be understood and used.*

Not too Detailed: *A requirement that is written on a suitable level of detail for the stakeholders to understand, without inhibiting the stakeholders' (e.g.,developers) creativity.*

Not-an-epic: *A requirement that is written on a level that is appropriate for the implementation work and testing.*

Well Structured *A requirement that is structured in a way that facilitates the work for other stakeholders (e.g., developers and testers).*

Terminology: *A requirement that is written with correct terminology as well as with terms that are used in correct way,*

Traceable: *A requirement that is easy to trace, even if it is in the future when the feature is completed, or the team has ended, been replaced, or moved on to another project/value stream*

Testable: *A requirement that is written in a way that removes the eases the writing of test cases.*

Easy to adjust: *A requirement that makes it easy to be adjust later in the work process (beyond development)*

Fig. 4. Codebook: Characteristics of "good" requirements, with codes and descriptions of "good" requirements. Opposite descriptions would characterize "bad" requirements.

changing parts of requirements after developers receive them if they are aware of those likely changes. Figure 4 presents the codebook with the description of the quality characteristics as discussed with the interviewees.

4.3   RQ2: How Does the Perceived Quality of Requirements Impact the Work of Practitioners of Software Development?

In general, participants experience that bad requirements cause delays in development, that activities take longer, and that they need to perform tasks that they perceive someone else should have done. One possible cause of these experiences is the need for more communication within the team or with other teams or stakeholders. The interviewees also reported that good requirements positively impact in general, e.g., on code quality, shorten development time, or improve work satisfaction. In contrast, bad requirements harm code quality, cost or work satisfaction. Figure 5 presents the codebook with the main themes that emerged from the interview transcript analysis regarding RQ2.

Effects of Good or Bad Requirements: Artefacts developed based on good/bad requirements are affected by their quality.

Difficulties when working with bad requirements: Some experience work with requirements to be easy, other moderate, other that it is difficult.

Communication good vs bad requirements: difference in communication when working with good vs bad requirements, e.g. increased need to contact different team members and stakeholders to find out lacking information from a bad requirement.

Reasons for bad requirements: The interviewee describes the reasons they have experienced that cause bad requirements as well as the reasons they speculate might cause bad requirements.

Feelings when working with requirements: The feelings that the interviewee experience when they work with requirements of different qualities, both good and bad.

Challenges with bad requirements: Development is delayed or parts of the process take longer time. They have to do work that (they perceive) someone else should have done.

Slow Process: The development process and/or its practices are considered time-consuming or slow. For instance, more time consuming compared to other companies or contexts.

Ripple effects: Changes to requirements, e.g. changed or added information, can have ripple effects in amount of work required by developers. For instance, requiring developers to track multiple artefacts, e.g. pull requests.

No bad requirements: The interviewee expresses not having experienced any bad requirements. (Does not mean that they does not change their mind during the interview)

View on Requirements: The interviewee expresses their view on requirements and their experience of other's views on requirements and any similarities or differences

Requirements Engineering Training: The training and education that the interviewee has with requirements engineering and the processes in creating requirements.

Changes on Requirements during development: Changes to quality of requirements, such as UX, look and feel, performance, text, or security, and how it affects the development and testing.

RQ2

Fig. 5. Codebook: Impact of the quality of requirements

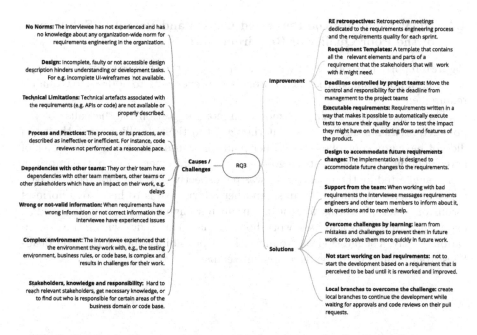

No Norms: The interviewee has not experienced and has no knowledge about any organization-wide norm for requirements engineering in the organization.

Design: Incomplete, faulty or not accessible design description hinders understanding or development tasks. For e.g. incomplete UI-wireframes not available.

Technical Limitations: Technical artefacts associated with the requirements (e.g. APIs or code) are not available or properly described.

Process and Practices: The process, or its practices, are described as ineffective or inefficient. For instance, code reviews not performed at a reasonable pace.

Dependencies with other teams: They or their team have dependencies with other team members, other teams or other stakeholders which have an impact on their work, e.g. delays

Wrong or not-valid information: When requirements have wrong information or not correct information the interviewee have experienced issues

Complex environment: The interviewee experienced that the environment they work with, e.g., the testing environment, business rules, or code base, is complex and results in challenges for their work.

Stakeholders, knowledge and responsibility: Hard to reach relevant stakeholders, get necessary knowledge, or to find out who is responsible for certain areas of the business domain or code base.

Causes / Challenges

RQ3

Improvement

Solutions

RE retrospectives: Retrospective meetings dedicated to the requirements engineering process and the requirements quality for each sprint.

Requirement Templates: A template that contains all the relevant elements and parts of a requirement that the stakeholders that will work with it might need.

Deadlines controlled by project teams: Move the control and responsibility for the deadline from management to the project teams

Executable requirements: Requirements written in a way that makes it possible to automatically execute tests to ensure their quality and/or to test the impact they might have on the existing flows and features of the product.

Design to accommodate future requirements changes: The implementation is designed to accommodate future changes to the requirements.

Support from the team: When working with bad requirements the interviewee messages requirements engineers and other team members to inform about it, ask questions and to receive help.

Overcome challenges by learning: learn from mistakes and challenges to prevent them in future work or to solve them more quickly in future work.

Not start working on bad requirements: not to start the development based on a requirement that is perceived to be bad until it is reworked and improved.

Local branches to overcome the challenge: create local branches to continue the development while waiting for approvals and code reviews on their pull requests.

Fig. 6. Codebook: Causes, solutions and improvements for "bad" requirements

Table 2. Mapping Codebook Characteristics to the ISO [10] and IREB [2] standards.

Codes from Codebook	ISO [10] Characteristics & Attributes	IREB [2] Characteristics & Attributes
Clear	Unambiguous, Comprehensible.	Unambiguous, Understandable
Concrete	-	-
Complete	Complete	Complete, Avoid incomplete conditions
Correct	Correct	-
Purpose	Necessary	Necessary
Feasible	-	-
Easy to adjust	-	-
Relevant for Stakeholders	Appropriate	-
Short Description	-	Short and well-structured sentences
Not-too-detailed	-	-
Well Structured	-	-
Terminology	Avoid open-ended non-verifiable terms, avoid subjective language	Defining and consistently using a uniform terminology, avoid vague or, ambiguous terms and phrases
Logical	-	-
Traceable	-	Traceable
Testable	Verifiable	Verifiable
Not-an-epic	-	-

4.4 RQ3: What are the Perceived Causes and Potential Solutions of the Poor Quality of Requirements?

Figure 6 reports the code book with descriptions of the themes related to causes, challenges, potential solutions and process improvements to address low-quality requirements.

The requirements engineers' most common suggestion for the cause of the poor requirements quality was that they got too tight deadlines that the team did not have any control over. Another plausible cause was stated to be a lack of agreement on what constitutes a good (or bad) requirement. One of the improvements suggested by the interviewees was retrospective meetings for requirements engineers between different teams. Another alternative is to have some form of forum or other platforms for the requirements engineers to share knowledge, experience, and ideas and have workshops to share knowledge within the organization. Lastly, a suggestion was to move the responsibility and control over deadlines from managers to the development teams.

5   Discussion

5.1   RQ1: How Do Software Development Practitioners Define Requirements Quality?

In this subsection, we discuss the main quality characteristics highlighted by the participants, mapping them to the quality characteristics included in the ISO [10] and IREB [2].

Table 2 shows the mapping between the different characteristics highlighted by the participants to the ones in the standards.

As mentioned in Sect. 4.2, most developers and testers agree that a requirement has to be complete when they receive it. However, some testers do not necessarily agree that the requirements must be complete when the developers receive them. Requirements engineers argue that requirements are artefacts that can change during development. Testers do not mind if changes occur, but when the functionality is implemented and sent to them for testing, the requirements should be complete so that they can be verified.

One developer expressed that they worked in a team with a requirement standard that did not require the requirements to be complete when the developers received them. Instead, the norm in this team was that the requirements engineer would perform their own investigations while developers worked on parts of the requirement that were considered to be "done". Similarly, other interviewees stated that working with incomplete requirements in their team was possible.

Some interviewees said that a requirement needs to give the stakeholders insight into the requirement's purpose and when it is considered done, i.e., the definition of done. Some quotes are "The ones that make developers understand the scope". "To understand the purpose of what we want to achieve". Hence, not only should the requirements describe the functionality but also the acceptance criteria.

One could argue that the requirements engineers should focus on domain knowledge and present requirements to the developers and testers that convey this knowledge. One participant expressed that the consequence of the lack of technical knowledge is that the requirements engineers do not know what is possible to implement and what is not, nor what limitations exist in one platform but not in another when they create features for both.

A subject that most interviewees brought up was that they perceived that a requirement should be written for the Stakeholders that will use it. "It depends on the developer, the business analyst or the tester how they want it written". "In our team are several different roles that should understand it; our APO [agile product owner] looks at different parts than what our developer does". Regarding how to deem a requirement, whether it is good or bad, a developer said: "Maybe it's not the ones that have the most insight in a user story [requirement] that should judge if it's ready for development, but maybe those that have lesser knowledge in the area are the better persons to ask if it's clear enough for them to understand what they are supposed to do". They base their subjective view on their technical and domain knowledge about the subject, which allows them to deal with assumptions more accurately.

5.2   RQ2: How Does the Perceived Quality of Requirements Impact the Work of Practitioners of Software Development?

Bad Requirements Require More Communication. Communication among requirements engineers, developers, testers, or other development teams, was the go-to practice for solving issues with the requirements for developers and testers. The logical outcome of this way of working is longer development time and an additional burden placed on the development team. A burden that could have been mitigated if the requirement had been better upfront. A developer stated, "Like I said earlier, a lot of the time that I want to put on programming is instead put on communication with BA:s [Business Analysts], UX [user experience] and other developers that have knowledge about what I'm working on. One does not develop so much; it is very much investigation work".

Most interviewees, independent of role, have described that communication is different when working with good requirements compared to working with bad ones. One of the most mentioned differences is that more communication is needed within the team or with other stakeholders when working with a requirement perceived as bad. As stated by one of the interviewees, "Bad requirements generally result in that the time you could have put into making a good requirement from the beginning is instead spent on setting up meetings or communicate *on the fly*".

Another consequence of bad requirements commonly mentioned was ripple effects. As expressed by one of the requirements engineers: "If I get questions [about a requirement] then I understand that I have forgotten something or haven't been clear with something. That will make it take more time, there will be user stories [requirements] that stays, sprint after sprint, and will have to be brought back to me for further investigations".

Another essential aspect is understanding of the area, domain and business rules for the requirements. This includes all the work connected to them, directly affecting the team's communication. A statement from the interviews was: "A lot of the understanding of a requirement is that you create a form of consensus. If you have a basic understanding of what needs to be done and how to solve it, then the requirements don't need to be formulated in the same way as if you didn't have it [the basic understanding]".

According to Zowghi and Nurmul [21], the more often developers and customers communicate during the RE process, the less volatile the requirements become. In the organization where this study was performed, the requirements engineers acted as product owners (customers).

Increased Workload and Doing Someone Else's Work. Participants described that additional work with incorrect information resulted in having

·to redo the work after correcting the information. The quality of the requirement impacts this challenge, e.g. a clear, well-written and complete requirement might be easier to implement and test than one where the information is faulty.

Bad requirements can cause ripple effects in overhead communication, especially incomplete requirements cause such ripple effects and increased workload. As stated by the interviewees: "This slows us down. So, it's kind of a joint work with the whole team, how we are coping with bad requirements, it's kind of more work for the developers then of course for the testers.", "Bad requirements create more work for us, testers because then we need to return to the business people, and the developers might have to rework something, so it leads to more work or rework". A severe consequence of receiving bad requirements is when a bad requirement is misunderstood by both developers and testers, implemented, and released. As expressed by one of the interviewees, "Then you realize that what came out in production is not correct, but we both [developer and tester] thought that it looked correct because 'that is how it should work', then it can end up very wrong". A requirements engineer said, "Sometimes one can write bad requirements, and it is developed according to them, and then you have to redo the work".

Four out of five requirements engineers have described those bad requirements they create also impact their work. The requirements engineer who did not experience an impact described that the questions did not impact them and that they viewed a part of their work as being prepared to explain the requirements to developers and testers. "You can foresee that you might get questions and that you are the one that will get the bad feedback on the requirements".

Interviewees experience not enough analysis performed on some of the requirements perceived as bad before handing them over to developers. In these cases, developers have to do work that they consider someone else should have done but which is required to overcome the lack in quality of the requirements. Most often, they need to perform investigations by going through documentation or contacting colleagues or other stakeholders, similar to what requirements engineers do when creating the requirements. The implications of this additional work are increased workload and work time in the development process, reduced work satisfaction and increased cost. Additionally, sometimes, the developers find out that someone else has to perform work before they can do anything leading to dependencies and blocking of requirements.

5.3   Effects on Morale

The Interviewees were asked to express how they feel when they work with bad and good requirements. We asked the requirements engineers how it feels to work with creating requirements. Three of them mentioned that, when working with challenging requirements or receiving requirements from stakeholders that they perceive are bad, they feel frustration, stress, anger, and exhaustion. "Exhausting is a word that comes to mind first". "It can be anger and understanding that some people don't have the same approach you have".

Two requirements engineers did not mention receiving bad requirements. However, when describing how it felt when they created challenging requirements, they experienced it to be educational but also challenging in a positive way as they learn from the challenge, "The challenge is in itself educational. I don't see it as something negative but rather something that I learn from". One of the reasons for the big difference in the positive and negative experiences of challenges when creating requirements could be related to the type of challenge they encountered. The challenges that the two requirements engineers described a positive view and feelings from working with challenging requirements were: (i) finding out stakeholders to contact for information; (ii) challenges with some terminology; (iii) how to get all the information from different sources together; and (vi) to write the requirements in a clear way for the developers and testers.

The three requirements engineers that had a negative experience when working with challenging requirements described challenges such as: (i) technical debt, e.g., legacy code, that affected the creation of requirements, (ii) that the test environment was perceived as unstable, (iii) that some areas of the organization do not have any clear owner, (iv) that legal and compliance aspects are difficult to work with, and (v) that the roadmap can be drastically changed without any heads-up by the managers.

When the requirements engineers are working with requirements they have made that the developers or testers perceive to be bad requirements, they describe that it feels sad and stressful, that it impacts their self-esteem, and that it drains their energy. "It results in that I feel more stressed, I get less good work done, and it affects one's own self-esteem". When working with requirements that they did not experience as challenging and when creating requirements that developers and testers perceived to be good, the requirements engineers describe it as fun and satisfying. Most testers described that they experienced stress, frustration, a feeling of disappointment or dissatisfaction, and a loss of interest when they worked with bad requirements. As stated by two interviewees: "When you have to talk with people, or when insecurity arises, you have to read it over and over again, you get frustrated. I lose interest if it is too bad"; "Frustrating, and stressful. I might be maybe angry, or I might be disappointed". They also explained that their work became less efficient and often resulted in more work because they had to communicate to other team members and often perform their tests again.

Feelings described by the interviewed developers when they received requirements they perceived as bad were: exhaustion, stress, frustration, a feeling of sadness, that they get feeling of doing something pointless, ineffective, and a waste of time, and that it was not fun when they worked with bad requirements. As stated by one interviewee: "Facepalm [interviewee put their hand on their forehead], it's a waste of time. Just a waste of time, resources, and energy", "One gets sad and feels simply unproductive. You want the hours you put down on your work to be meaningful". On the contrary, in general, the developers said they experienced positive feelings and that more work was done when they worked with good requirements. One from each of the two developer groups, newly employed developers and developers that have worked for at least a few years, said they were not negatively emotionally affected by the bad requirements. One interviewee stated: "Business as usual [laughing]. You can usually do something about bad requirements before you start working on them". Still, one of the interviewees described strong positive feelings when working with good requirements, "Effective. It's stronger feelings when you have a clear good requirement that you can just work through".

It is generally believed that morale has an impact on productivity. However, it has been difficult to prove in software engineering since both morale and productivity are difficult to measure [19,20]. Work morale can also affect a company's attraction and retention of employees. One possible consequence of lowered work morale could be that employees decide to leave the organization, "Our developers are the ones that produce something of value, and if they are angry or sad over something that was possible to go live with, then we risk losing them. To onboard new developers is not a bed of roses". The quality of requirements that a requirements engineer work with might affect their and other Stakeholders' morale. However, work morale can also be affected by more factors such as work environment or compensation.

5.4   RQ3: What are the Perceived Causes and Potential Solutions of the Poor Quality of Requirements?

Potential Causes for Poor Quality Requirements. The organization has not adopted any norms for good requirements, and none of the interviewees had heard or experienced any form of such organization-wide norms or standards. However, several shared courses in the subject are available to the organization's employees. One requirements engineer said: "I have covered the ones that come with the courses introduced in this company from different phases, such as 'simplify', 'SWAP', and now 'SAFE'". The closest to a shared norm that a few interviewees mentioned was 'SWAP' and the branching that derives from it, "What we can lean on is 'SWAP' and the different branches that derive from it. But I wouldn't say that there is any statement of 'this is how you structure requirements at this company'. It is more from team to team".

A developer whose team requires that all requirements have to be complete before the developers receive them and that no changes are allowed, stated that they experienced that they still got incomplete requirements. He perceives a lack of knowledge or information by the requirements engineers. "Then we [the developers] need to step in and explain technically what is possible and what is not for the different platforms. It results in us more or less educating our requirements engineers". This statement highlights a possible root cause of the low quality of requirements, i.e., the requirements engineers lack technical knowledge.

Potential Solutions and Improvements. Some interviewees had suggestions for how to solve the different causes for bad requirements that have arisen in the interviews. One of the long-term solutions is to enable more communication between requirements engineers across the organization in some form of platform. One example given was to have retrospective meetings between requirements engineers, another to have a forum dedicated to RE, and a third would be to have a form of meeting for sharing knowledge, similar to tech talks that developers have. As a complement to introducing a knowledge-sharing platform for requirements engineers, one could argue that a norm for creating requirements should be shared across the organization. This use of RE forums could be especially beneficial for organizations with several requirements engineers with different backgrounds and knowledge of requirements engineering, similar to the studied organization. One possibility is that such norms might naturally be developed and polished by the practitioners as a consequence of the activities and sharing of the knowledge-sharing platform. Another suggestion from interviewees as a short-term solution was to move the control of the deadlines for projects that development teams worked on to the development teams. Thus, the requirements do not get rushed and enable a more agile way of working since fixed deadlines are more an aspect of the waterfall principles. However, one can speculate that such a change in the organization might be costly should the deadlines be moved forward repeatedly with delayed releases. Nevertheless, one can also argue that it can ease the quality assurance process. In addition, the practitioners would be less stressed and feel more work satisfaction. Hopefully, there should be fewer defects and less rework, possibly covering the extra cost that allows development teams to move deadlines forward might bring.

The expressed need for a platform dedicated to knowledge sharing between requirements engineers could indicate that the organization might benefit from an organization-wide norm for requirements engineering. However, many interviewees expressed a strong willingness to have flexibility and freedom in their work and their team's ways of working. Therefore it should be considered to ensure that such a norm will be kept on a supporting level that does not encroach on the practitioners' creativity.

Almost all interviewees, if not all, concur that if the organization experience more significant benefits to not having a standard norm, an improvement that the organization already should consider is a platform for knowledge sharing between requirements engineers. Imposing an organization-wide norm can hinder autonomy and heterogeneousness in the teams' ways of working.

There are several possibilities for how this platform could take shape. A straightforward example could be to have a forum dedicated to the RE-process and encouragement to the requirements engineers to use it and share the knowledge amongst themselves. Another example could be to have something like the tech talks developers have, in which they can share news, knowledge, and insights. Some requirements engineers interviewed also asked for retrospectives for the requirements process, which they experienced a lack of. The participants also suggested the use of templates and quality gates for requirements (i.e., not starting to work with low-quality requirements until they reach a certain quality level) as potential solutions to mitigate the effects of low-quality requirements.

6   Threats to Validity

This section discusses threats to validity from four perspectives: construct validity, external validity, and reliability.

Construct Validity. Construct validity is concerned with whether the studied measures reflect the constructs the researcher has in mind and what is stated in the research questions. The first author designed the flexible interview protocol and then reviewed it with the second and third authors. We acknowledge that the participants do not include all the relevant stakeholders in the organization. We tried mitigating this threat by involving participants with different roles and varying expertise from the companies.

External Validity concerns the extent to which the findings can be generalized outside of the studied case and whether they apply to other organizations. One of the misunderstandings about case study research is the inability to generalize from a single case [8]. However, we have tried to build a theory to understand requirements quality, the impact of low-quality requirements, and causes and potential solutions by building analytic generalization through theories instead of gaining statistical generalizabilty. We have provided the characteristics of the case under analysis to allow us to evaluate its generalizability. However, still, further replications are needed to verify the results.

Reliability concerns whether the data and analysis are independent of the researchers. To increase the reliability, the second and third authors validated the coding scheme and the coding process by independently coding an interview transcript. The results of this independent coding matched for 74% of the codes.

7   Conclusions and Further Work

In this paper, we have presented an interview study to analyze how: (i) practitioners from different roles define good and bad requirements; (ii) how the quality of the requirements impacts their work; and (iii) what might be the causes for poor quality requirements, as well as potential solutions and improvements.

The results regarding the quality characteristics for requirements show that, although all interviewees agree that requirements should be clear, there is a wide range of views regarding the need to work with complete requirements. The participants highlighted that, in general, they experienced negative emotions, more work, and overhead communication when they worked with requirements they perceived to be of low quality. The participants suggested Requirements Engineering retrospectives, the use of templates, and quality gates for requirements (i.e., not starting to work with low-quality requirements until they reach a certain quality level) as potential improvements and solutions for low-quality requirements. Participants also suggested creating a requirements engineering forum (or guild) to disseminate requirements engineering knowledge better.

The most relevant further work is the replication of this study in other organizations to verify the results. Our preliminary results highlight some improvement areas that could be explored through longitudinal case studies or action research. Examples of those areas are the effects of establishing a knowledge-sharing forum for requirements engineers in organizations; or evaluating the cost, risk, and benefits of moving the control of deadlines from management to development teams in agile software development companies. These research areas could bring relevant results for researchers and software development organizations.

Acknowledgements. This research was supported by the KKS foundation through the SHADE KKS Hög project (Ref: 20170176) and through the KKS SERT Research Profile project (Ref. 2018010) Blekinge Institute of Technology.

References

1. Braun, V., Clarke, V.: Using thematic analysis in psychology. Qualit. Res. Psychol. **3**, 77–101 (2006). https://doi.org/10.1191/1478088706qp063oa
2. Bühne, S., Glinz, M., van Louenhoud, H., Staal, S.: IREB Certified Professional for Requiremetns Engineering. CPRE Foundation Level - Syllabus. Standard, IREB, Karlsruhue, Germany (2022). https://www.ireb.org/content/downloads/2-cpre-foundation-level-syllabus-3-0/cpre_foundationlevel_syllabus_en_v.3.1.pdf
3. Cruzes, D.S., Dybå, T.: Recommended steps for thematic synthesis in software engineering. In: International Symposium on Empirical Software Engineering and Measurement, Banff, AB, Canada, pp. 275–284 (2011)
4. Damian, D., Chisan, J.: An empirical study of the complex relationships between requirements engineering processes and other processes that lead to payoffs in productivity, quality, and risk management. IEEE Trans. Softw. Eng. **32**(7), 433–453 (2006). https://doi.org/10.1109/TSE.2006.61
5. Ernst, N., Kazman, R., Delange, J.: Technical Debt in Practice: How to Find It and Fix It. MIT Press, Cambridge (2021)
6. Femmer, H., Fernández, D.M., Wagner, S., Eder, S.: Rapid quality assurance with requirements smells. J. Syst. Softw. **123**, 190–213 (2017). https://doi.org/10.1016/j.jss.2016.02.047
7. Femmer, H., Vogelsang, A.: Requirements quality is quality in use. IEEE Softw. **36**, 83–91 (2019). https://doi.org/10.1109/MS.2018.110161823
8. Flyvbjerg, B.: Five misunderstandings about case-study research. Qual. Inq. **12**, 219–245 (2006). https://doi.org/10.1177/1077800405284363
9. Frattini, J., Montgomery, L., Fischbach, J., Unterkalmsteiner, M., Mendez, D., Fucci, D.: A live extensible ontology of quality factors for textual requirements. In: 30th IEEE International Requirements Engineering Conference, pp. 274–280 (2022)
10. ISO/IEC/IEEE: ISO/IEC/IEEE 29148:2018 international standard - systems and software engineering - lifecycle processes - requirements engineering. Standard, ISO/IEC/IEEE, Geneva, CH (2018)
11. Javed, T., Maqsood, M.E., Durrani, Q.S.: A study to investigate the impact of requirements instability on software defects. ACM-SIGSOFT Softw. Eng. Notes **29**(3), 1–7 (2004). https://doi.org/10.1145/986710.986727
12. Kamata, M.I., Tamai, T.: How does requirements quality relate to project success or failure? In: 15th IEEE International Requirements Engineering Conference (RE 2007), pp. 69–78 (2007)

13. Lenberg, P., Feldt, R., Wallgren, L.G.: Towards a behavioral software engineering. In: Proceedings of the 7th International Workshop on Cooperative and Human Aspects of Software Engineering. ACM, Hyderabad (2014)

14. Linåker, J., Sulaman, S.M., Höst, M., Mello, R.M.D.: Guidelines for conducting surveys in software engineering v. 1.1. Technical report, Department of Computer Science, Lund University, Lund, Sweden (2015)

15. Meier, A., Kropp, M., Anslow, C., Biddle, R.: Stress in agile software development: practices and outcomes. In: Garbajosa, J., Wang, X., Aguiar, A. (eds.) XP 2018. LNBIP, vol. 314, pp. 259–266. Springer, Cham (2018). https://doi.org/10.1007/978-3-319-91602-6_18

16. Fernández, D.M., et al.: Naming the pain in requirements engineering. Empir. Softw. Eng. **22**(5), 2298–2338 (2016). https://doi.org/10.1007/s10664-016-9451-7

17. Mendez, D.: Supporting requirements-engineering research that industry needs: the NaPiRE initiative. IEEE Softw. **35**, 112–116 (2017). https://doi.org/10.1109/MS.2017.4541045

18. Rempel, P., Mäder, P.: Preventing defects: the impact of requirements traceability completeness on software quality. IEEE Trans. Softw. Eng. **43**(8), 777–797 (2017). https://doi.org/10.1109/TSE.2016.2622264

19. Storey, M.A., Zimmermann, T., Bird, C., Czerwonka, J., Murphy, B., Kalliamvakou, E.: Towards a theory of software developer job satisfaction and perceived productivity. IEEE Trans. Softw. Eng. **47**, 2125–2142 (2021). https://doi.org/10.1109/TSE.2019.2944354

20. Weakliem, D.L., Frenkel, S.J.: Morale and workplace performance. Work Occup. **33**, 335–361 (2016). https://doi.org/10.1177/0730888406290054

21. Zowghi, D., Nurmuliani, N.: A study of the impact of requirements volatility on software project performance. In: Proceedings - Asia-Pacific Software Engineering Conference, APSEC, pp. 3–11. IEEE, Gold Coast (2002)

Software Defect Prediction

Outlier Mining Techniques for Software Defect Prediction

Tim Cech[1]([envelope]) [iD], Daniel Atzberger[1], Willy Scheibel[1] [iD], Sanjay Misra[2] [iD], and Jürgen Döllner[1]

[1] Hasso Plattner Institute, Digital Engineering Faculty, University of Potsdam, Potsdam, Germany
{tim.cech,daniel.atzberger,willy.scheibel,
juergen.doellner}@hpi.uni-potsdam.de
[2] Department of Computer Science and Communication, Østfold University College, Halden, Norway
sanjay.misra@hiof.no

Abstract. Using software metrics as a method of quantification of software, various approaches were proposed for locating defect-prone source code units within software projects. Most of these approaches rely on supervised learning algorithms, which require labeled data for adjusting their parameters during the learning phase. Usually, such labeled training data is not available. Unsupervised algorithms do not require training data and can therefore help to overcome this limitation.

In this work, we evaluate the effect of unsupervised learning by means of cluster-based algorithms and outlier mining algorithms for the task of defect prediction, i.e., locating defect-prone source code units. We investigate the effect of various class balancing and feature compressing techniques as preprocessing steps and show how sliding windows can be used to capture time series of source code metrics. We evaluate the Isolation Forest and Local Outlier Factor, as representants of outlier mining techniques. Our experiments on three publicly available datasets, containing a total of 11 software projects, indicate that the consideration of time series can improve static examinations by up to 3%. The results further show that supervised algorithms can outperform unsupervised approaches on all projects. Among all unsupervised approaches, the Isolation Forest achieves the best accuracy on 10 out of 11 projects.

Keywords: Software Defect Prediction · Unsupervised Learning · Outlier Mining

1 Introduction

Software defects reduce the added value for the customer or lead to an increased effort in development if they have to be corrected later in development [31]. Therefore, the timely detection of defective source code units is a central theme of code quality. Classically, *unit tests* and *integration tests* are used for the early detection of defective code units by testing the respective units for their functionality [32].

D. Mendez et al. (Eds.): SWQD 2023, LNBIP 472, pp. 41–60, 2023.
https://doi.org/10.1007/978-3-031-31488-9_3

In practice, however, it is often untenable to test all functionalities, or the potential for defects is not yet known to the developers at the time the software is developed. Software metrics, which describe various aspects of the complexity and quality of the source code, can be used complementary to monitoring the development of large software systems. A distinction is made between static code metrics and process metrics. Static code metrics, such as *Lines of Code* (LOC), *McCabe Complexity* (MCCC), or *Nesting Level* (NL), measure aspects of a software project at a specific point in time, i.e., a source code revision. In contrast, process metrics describe the change between two revisions, e.g., the number of developers involved in a commit or the number of changed LOC [42]. Based on those metrics, statistical analyses can be applied to locate defect-prone source code units [21].

Various *Machine Learning* (ML) techniques have been used for detecting defect-prone source code units using software metrics. Most approaches use supervised ML techniques on static code metrics of a single revision [21,31]. Supervised approaches require a labeled training dataset, which is challenging to obtain, since usually no records of the defect history that can be used for labeling are kept [3,29]. In this case, another approach is desirable, that does not require the project to have a history of labeled defects. We focus on the usage of unsupervised training techniques, which were investigated recently to overcome this issue [27,37,39]. Previous research with unsupervised methods indicates that even basic approaches provide acceptable results [37]. However, in general, they achieve weaker results compared to supervised techniques [16]. Recent results by Moshtari et al. show that the distribution of defects within a software project follows the Pareto principle, i.e., a small fraction of the source code units contain a large part of the defects [27]. Furthermore, defective source code units are also distinct from non-defective code units in terms of metrics and can therefore be treated as outliers [27].

Motivated by this result, we extend the work of Moshtari et al. to time series of metrics by comparing unsupervised learning algorithms by means of cluster-based algorithms and outlier mining algorithms with basic supervised approaches. For it, we want to study if any approach is superior to others. Subsequently, we will not address questions about the nature of defects but inherit their definitions from the creators of each dataset. We describe each source code unit by a sequence of software metrics using sliding windows and a subsequent feature compression technique. We then apply the respective defect prediction algorithm to locate defect-prone source code units. In summary, we make the following contributions:

1. We present a computational experiment comparing basic supervised, cluster-based techniques and outlier techniques addressing common pitfalls by Feature Compression and Class Balancing.
2. We present the use of sliding windows for modeling a time series of software metrics.
3. We introduce the application of the Isolation Forest and Local Outlier Factor, as examples of outlier mining algorithms, for the task of locating defect-prone source code units.

4. We present an evaluation pipeline for comparing unsupervised and supervised defect prediction algorithms, and conduct experiments on three publicly available datasets for a total of 11 software projects.

The remainder of this work is structured as follows: Sect. 2 studies related work on defect prediction techniques. In Sect. 3, we elaborate on our approach. The computational experiment to investigate the research questions above are detailed in Sect. 4 and the results are presented in the Sect. 5. We conclude with a discussion and possible threats to validity in Sect. 6 and suggest conclusions and future work in Sect. 7.

2   Related Work

Supervised and unsupervised approaches can be distinguished in the field of ML. We focus on unsupervised software defect prediction, and thus, study the related work for unsupervised models in more detail. In contrast, we only give a high-level view of the field of supervised defect prediction. Additionally, many preprocessing methods were already evaluated in the literature, showing that the choice of the combination of the most adequate preprocessing method and model is non-trivial [4,35].

Unsupervised Approaches. Yang et al. were one of the first who applied unsupervised learning techniques for effort-aware defect prediction [39]. Effort-aware defect prediction describes the attempt to predict defects while taking into account the effort required to check them. Based on their results, the authors suggest that (basic) unsupervised models can outperform supervised models in terms of recall when taking the file size, and therefore the effort of units that need to be reviewed, into account. In subsequent research, this effect was put into perspective by Fu and Menzies as well as Huang et al. [12,16]. Before, Nam and Kim already argued that unsupervised approaches can be beneficial because they do not need historical training data, which can be hard to obtain for defect prediction [29].

Subsequently, several studies were conducted exploring different, more complex unsupervised approaches for defect prediction. Albahli combines several (also unsupervised) models resulting in an accuracy of 81% on a dataset containing seven open-source projects [2]. Xu et al. reviewed 40 cluster-based approaches and observed that these achieve similar results to typical supervised approaches [37]. Zhang et al. also found that unsupervised models are competitive to supervised models that were trained on another project [40].

Studies on 16 software projects by Moshtari et al. showed that the distribution of defects over a software project follows the Pareto principle, i.e., a large part of the defects is contained in a small part of the units [27]. Assuming that the defective units also differ significantly from the majority concerning their metrics, the localization of defects can be considered an outlier problem. Moshtari et al. investigated the use of five proximity-based outlier mining techniques. The best results were achieved using the *k nearest neighbor* (kNN) algorithm.

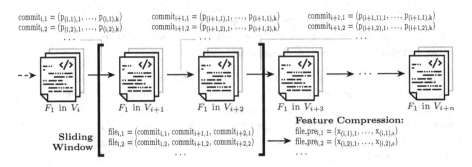

Fig. 1. An example visualization for our preprocessing pipeline on process metrics. The process metrics that describe the change between revision i and $i+1$ in File$_j$ are given by commit$_{i,j} = (p_{(i,j),1}, \ldots, (p_{(i,j),k})$. The process metrics of three commits of File F_j are collected in the vector file$_{i,j} = ($commit$_{i,j}$, commit$_{i+1,j}$, commit$_{i+2,j})$. The compressed vector describing F_j is given by file_pre$_{i,j} = (x_{(i,j),1}, \ldots, x_{(i,j),s})$.

Supervised Approaches. Several literature reviews were conducted, e.g., by Rathore et al., Li et al., and Wahono, summarizing various supervised approaches in different use-cases with different metrics and models [21,31]. Liu et al. already considered a time series of code and process metrics for defect prediction [23]. By training a *Recurrent Neural Network* (RNN) on nine projects of the PROMISE dataset [34], the new model was able to outperform basic models using code and process metrics in terms of cost-effectiveness, the Schott-Knott-Test, and Win/Tie/Loss. Another recently studied approach is the usage of *Cross Project Defect Prediction* (CPDP) [3]. Here, the defect prediction model is trained on another project, which has labeled data available. After the completion of the training phase, the model tries to predict defects in the target project. CPDP has only achieved limited success [3,42]. Yan et al. discovered that for a certain dataset, unsupervised within-project defect prediction outperforms supervised CPDP models [38].

Data Preprocessing. Several studies were conducted concerning the general pre-processing steps required before creating the actual defect prediction model. Mende provides a general overview of several pitfalls and aspects that should be considered when constructing a model for defect prediction [25]. In this work, we focus on a selected subset of those aspects, namely feature compression techniques for all models and balancing techniques for supervised models. Kondo et al. suggest that supervised models profit most from techniques that filter metrics, therefore preserving the original meaning [19]. In contrast, unsupervised models profited most from synthetic methods that combine several original metrics in a new synthetic one. Zhu et al. support the claim that Autoencoder can be a useful feature compression technique [41]. Another aspect of preprocessing is concerned with the question of how to handle imbalanced datasets, which are typical for defect prediction tasks [27]. Tantithamthavorn et al. investigated that the choice of the balancing technique is non-trivial and should be considered carefully [35].

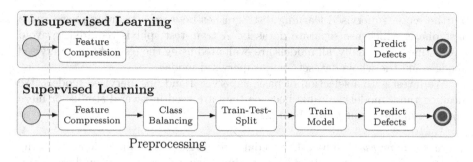

Fig. 2. Comparing the workflow for defect prediction with an unsupervised vs. supervised model. The workflow with an unsupervised model is much simpler because the imbalance of the dataset, overfitting, and the requirement of labels are not an issue.

This result is supported by Mahmood et al. who also investigated the effect of imbalance on the performance of supervised defect predictors [24].

3   Data Preprocessing and Modeling

In this section, we detail our approach for locating defect-prone source code units by using unsupervised learning algorithms on time series of source code metrics. Assuming that defects differ significantly in their metrics from non-defective samples, we adopt the idea of Moshtari et al. and apply outlier techniques for locating defect-prone source code units [27]. For this purpose, we additionally adopt an idea from Ding et al., who demonstrated in another use case that a *sliding window* can be used to capture an evolution of metrics to improve the quality of outlier mining [10]. This results in the basic workflow shown in Fig. 1.

Sliding Windows. Sliding windows are a technique known from stream data processing to analyze data-intensive data streams [9], i.e., several data samples are combined and viewed coherently [10]. For example, instead of just investigating metrics between two commits, all the changes in two consecutive commits are gathered into one feature vector. If, for example, five different process metrics are considered and the *Window Size* (WS) is three, then each file or sample is represented by a 15-dimensional vector. As this results in a high-dimensional vector, we apply feature compression techniques to reduce the size of the feature vector to overcome the *Curse of Dimensionality* [36].

Processing Pipeline. After gathering the data in an high-dimensional feature space using sliding windows, we preprocess the data to prepare them for prediction. Figure 2 compares the different preprocessing and prediction pipelines for supervised and unsupervised learning. Both pipelines are including the task of feature compression. Afterwards, as Bennin et al. showed for supervised techniques, the balancing of the defect and non-faulty class is desirable [4]. Since unsupervised techniques do not inherently distinguish between faulty and non-faulty samples, this preprocessing step is only applicable to supervised learning.

Furthermore, supervised learning distinguishes between a training phase and a test phase, which use separate datasets. A train-test split is required to avoid overfitting [13]. Finally, all models are evaluated using the test set for supervised models and the whole dataset for unsupervised models.

We investigate a selection of basic supervised and unsupervised models. We deemed those models suitable because they are used in several studies or more complex models built upon them [21,37].

Feature Compression. The gathered data suffers from high dimensionality. Many models produce worse results on a high-dimensional space, as the number of samples required to generalize grows exponentially with the number of features. This effect is denoted as the Curse of Dimensionality [36]. To avoid this, an additional preprocessing step transfers the data samples to a lower-dimensional space as shown in Fig. 1. In addition, Jiarpakdee et al. also suggest that even if the feature vector in and of itself is not already very high-dimensional, it may still be worthwhile to remove features [17]. Especially removing high correlations of individual variables from the data is usually desirable. Substantial differences can be observed between supervised and unsupervised learning techniques regarding Feature Compression [19]. For example, supervised learning predictors favor those techniques that preserve the original context of the metrics. This is also desirable in terms of the interpretability of the model. Unsupervised learning methods would benefit in particular from those techniques that construct new synthetic features from the given features. In this work, we focus on the following feature selection and synthesization techniques: The *Variance Inflation Factor* (VIF) [26], *Autoencoders* (AE) [19,41], and *Feature agglomeration* (FA). FA refers to a technique to filter correlated variables by repeated clustering. Metrics are merged if they are highly correlated leading to a more dense clustering.

Class Balancing. For supervised learning techniques, it can be beneficial to balance between the defect (faulty) class and a non-defect (non-faulty) class in the training dataset [4]. This is especially true since the defect class usually follows the Pareto principle [27]. Tantithamthavorn et al. found that the choice of a balancing technique has a significant impact onto the classification result, thus different upsampling techniques may lead to different results [35]. We considered three different upsampling techniques: *Synthetic Minority Over-sampling Technique* (SMOTE) [8], the *MAHAKIL* algorithm [5] and an *Euclidean Noise* (EN) technique. EN is a quick-to-execute naive technique. New samples are generated by offsetting each sample of the defect class with a noise signal drawn from a normal distribution.

Supervised Learning Techniques. Supervised learning is divided in a training and a test phase. In the training phase, labeled data is used for learning an abstraction of the data, which is subsequently used for predicting unseen data. We consider the following supervised learning techniques: *Random Forest* (RF), *Support Vector Machines* (SVM), *Logistic Regression* (LR), *Naive Bayes* (NB)

Table 1. An overview about the investigated datasets. LOC refers to the lines of code metric, P means project, and FPP means files per project. The Unified GitHub dataset and Jureczko only report on versions of projects with no specific time-frame stated.

Dataset	# P	# FPP	Time Frame	Type Metrics	jit Metric
Change Burst	1	6 728	One week	Process	Changed LOC
Unified GitHub	10	≈ 1,000	Sporadic	Static & Process	LOC
Jureczko	13	max. 250	Sporadic	Static	LOC

model, and *Multi-Layer Perceptron* (MLP) [33]. In addition, we combine the models above to an *Ensemble* (ES) with majority voting as the final decision rule.

Unsupervised Learning Techniques. In contrast to supervised learning, unsupervised learning does not distinguish between a training and test phase, because no labels are involved when applying them to data. Since labels are not used for unsupervised learning, we assigned which detected structure in our dataset is identified with the faulty class and the non-faulty class. We identify the smaller structure (fewer samples belong to the structure) as the cluster of the faulty class, since the number of defects is usually smaller [27]. We only had to make an exception for the *mcMMO* project, where the situation is reversed.

We consider two different unsupervised learning approaches. First, we use cluster-based techniques, which were previously already investigated e.g. by Xu et al. [37] or Li et al. [20]. Second, we additionally use the property found by Moshtari et al. that the metrics of defective source code units often have exceptional values [27]. Therefore outlier mining techniques are applicable.

Cluster-based techniques create clusters according to a criterion defined by the model, e.g., the density or similarity of sample regions. In contrast to Moshtari et al., we only investigate cluster-based techniques that allow us to set the number of clusters to the number of our target classes (defect and non-defect) [27]. Specifically, we study the following cluster-based techniques: The *k-Means* (kM) algorithm with $k = 2$, because our target has two classes [37] and the MeanShift (MS) algorithm with orphans [14]. Orphans are samples that do not belong to any density structure or would significantly change the density structure of the detected clusters if they were forcibly assigned to a cluster [14]. We identify the orphans as faulty samples and the remaining structures as non-faulty samples.

In contrast, outlier mining describes another set of techniques that focus on the process of detecting conspicuous data samples, i.e., to identify anomalies in the given dataset. Outliers are characterized as samples that are significant dissimilar to the majority of samples. So, outlier mining rather investigates dissimilarities in the dataset instead of similarities like cluster-based techniques. We investigate the following outlier mining techniques: The *Local Outlier Factor* (LOF) and an *Isolation Forest* (IF) [22].

4   Computational Experiment

We evaluate our basic models with the pipeline described in Sect. 3 on the *Change Burst* dataset [28], the *Unified GitHub* dataset [11], and the *Jureczko* dataset [18]. Our data pipeline is based on *scikit-learn*[1] and *Tensorflow with Keras*[2] library in Python. Those libraries are implementing all our investigated basic models as well as our preprocessing techniques, excluded the SMOTE and MAHAKIL algorithm for which the implementation is given in the auxiliary material. We evaluate our results in terms of precision, recall, F_1-score, accuracy as well as a *Just-in-time-accuracy* (JIT-accuracy). For consistency, we set the random seed to 42 to make our results deterministic and repeatable. For supervised models, we used a stratified train-test-split: 60% of the data was used for training and the remaining 40% for testing. From now on, we refer to a model as a specific combination of a basic supervised or unsupervised such as RF, with a feature compression—for all basic models—and a class balancing technique —for supervised models only. According to the no-free-lunch-theorem the outcome of a classification result is generally data dependent, so the evaluation on more than one project and set of metrics is necessary [1]. Therefore, for a reliable evaluation, we used the three previously mentioned publicly available datasets. For each dataset, one file of a project is considered as one sample (file-level).

We summarized our datasets in Table 1. In detail, we used the following datasets:

- The Change Burst dataset contains process metrics, hence change rates between two commits for the *Eclipse* project [28]. A so called *Burst* represents the changes during a week. We have chosen the first *Gap* containing 10 bursts, since only few defects are fixed or newly introduced into the code, providing a stample number of samples for each class (faulty and non-faulty).
- The Unified GitHub dataset captures a wide variety of both static and process-oriented metrics for more than ten projects [11]. In contrast to the Change Burst dataset, the reported revisions are further apart in time (for details, cf. auxiliary material), therefore a number of files are created or deleted between two revisions. Therefore, the number of faulty and non-faulty samples is more volatile. We will only examine projects which report at least two defective modules over all revisions, because with no or only one defective module the SMOTE and MAHAKIL technique is not applicable. Also, it is impossible to learn any abstraction from exactly one example.
- Lastly, the Jureczko dataset offers a small collection of metrics for a larger number of projects [18].

The Change Burst dataset allows the most stable evaluation, because the number of files is constant and also the number of faulty and non-faulty samples is comparably constant. We will also test our findings on the Unified GitHub dataset. The Jureczko dataset has the most disadvantageous characteristics to

[1] https://scikit-learn.org.
[2] https://www.tensorflow.org/ and https://keras.io/.

allow a meaningful evaluation because it suffers from the same problems as the Unified GitHub dataset, i.e., the sample size total and per class is changing often and only reports on a small number of metrics. We therefore provide the results for the Jureczko dataset only in the auxiliary material for additional validation of our findings.

Quality Measures. Bowes et al. argued that such metrics should be used from which the original confusion matrix can be derived easily [7]. Therefore, we choose precision and recall for both classes as well as the weighted average. Additionally, we captured the F_1-scores for the positive and negative class. Furthermore, we captured two kinds of accuracy metrics. The classic accuracy is defined as the ratio between the sum of true positives and true negatives divided by the number of samples.

In addition, we define a JIT-accuracy (acc_{jit}). Let S be the set of all samples. Then, let $TP \subseteq S$ denote the set of all true positives, let $TN \subseteq S$ denote the set of all true negatives and let $f(s)$ be a mapping from the sample to the reciprocal normalized lines of (changed) code of the sample *((Changed) LOC)*, then the JIT-accuracy is given by:

$$acc_{jit} = \frac{\sum_{s \in TP \cup TN} s \cdot f(s)}{\sum_{t \in S} t \cdot f(t)}$$

This is to favor classifications that identify small faulty samples correctly and penalize results that incorrectly suggest a particularly large change for review. By determining precision, recall, and F_1-score for each of the classes, we show how well the predictor can handle the individual classes, and to that extent we circumvent the criticism of these values that is raised by Powers [30] or Hemmati et al. [15], for example.

Optimization of Hyperparameters. Unlike unsupervised models, supervised models usually need to be optimized during training time since they use a set of hyperparamaters [6]. For optimization, we use a random search with 50 iterations and five stratified validation folds [6]. We had to make an exception for SVMs, since their training time can be exhaustive depending on the choice of hyperparameters, therefore they are only optimized with five iterations and three folds. We have reported the full list of optimized attributes in our auxiliary material.

Additionally, we have to determine a WS for gathering the data (cf. Sect. 3). We used a *Grid Search* for optimization of this hyperparameter with the integer values 1–10 [6]. A WS of 1 means, that the model does not profit from the windowing aspect of our approach. We gathered data with according WS of 1–10 and let the models predict the defects in the next revision. We have chosen 10 as an upper bound since a burst in the ChangeBurst dataset contains ten revisions and no project in the Unified GitHub dataset report metrics for more than ten revisions for gathering and one for testing for a total of eleven revisions. In case of WS = 10 for the ChangeBurst dataset, the target variable is derived from the first revision of the second burst. Since a significant number of files is deleted

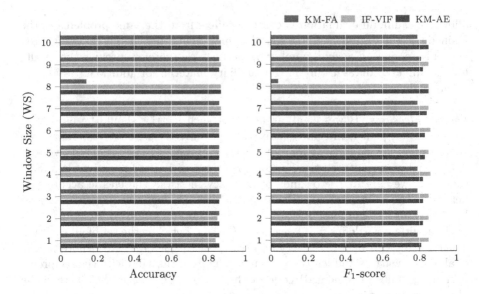

Fig. 3. Comparing WS by accuracy and F_1-score for the Eclipse project. The usage of a sliding window can improve the quality of unsupervised models by 1–3%. The positive effect is already visible if we use WS = 2.

and created between revisions for projects from the Unified GitHub dataset, we only evaluated on files that are present in all revisions. Since the Change Burst dataset captures the metrics more timely, only few files are created or deleted between revisions. The number of samples overall and per-class is more stable.

5 Results

We collect results regarding three questions. First we consider which influence the choice of the WS has on the performance of our models. Regarding the second question, we examine which supervised or unsupervised model performs best for multiple projects. We investigate the ten projects from the Unified GitHub dataset and one burst from the Change Burst dataset for Eclipse for a total of 11 projects. The third question compares the performance of supervised and unsupervised models. Again, we examine our 11 projects and the Eclipse project in more detail.

In general, we only consider results, if they can exceed a F_1-score of 10% in the faulty class, because models that show worse results do not provide an useful abstraction for finding defects, which is the main task in this paper. For completeness, however, those results are included in the auxiliary material.

5.1 Choice of the Window Size

We can observe two kinds of behavior when varying the WS of our sliding window. On the one hand, Fig. 3 shows the standard case that we observed for our

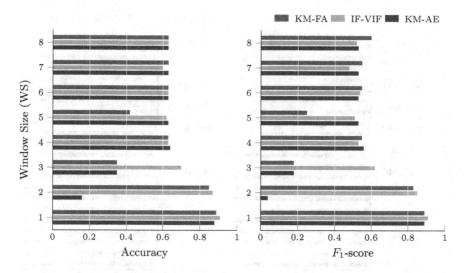

Fig. 4. For the hazelcast project the usage of a sliding window decreases the quality of unsupervised models. For WS = 2 the effect is comparatively small, but the loss in quality increases for larger WS.

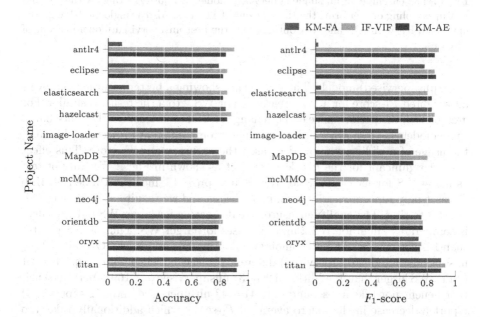

Fig. 5. The IF with VIF shows the best or one of the best accuracy for 10 out of 11 software projects and best F_1-scores for 8 out of 11 software projects. k-Means is better for the Android-Universal-Image-Loader (image-loader).

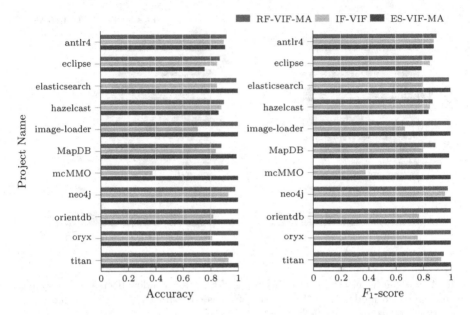

Fig. 6. The ensemble of all single supervised models (majority voting) with VIF and MA upsampling outperforms the IF in 11 out of 11 cases. Also a single model, e.g., the optimized RF with VIF and MA outperforms the best unsupervised model in 8 out of 11 cases.

(here unsupervised) models. The models are showing a better accuracy and overall weighted F_1-score for a WS greater 1. For WS 2 to 5 the result is similar. For greater WS, the performance do not change or became worse. On the other hand, some models have shown a different behavior on a different project. In this case, the usage of a sliding window decreased the accuracy and F_1-score. This effect is most significant for the *hazelcast* project as shown in Fig. 4. We can not test as many WS for hazelcast as for the Eclipse project, since the Unified GitHub Dataset only reports metrics for nine revisions and we require at least one revision for testing. The quality measures are decreasing for larger WS but the effect is comparably small for WS 2 and increases for larger WS. Thus, a WS greater than 1 is not beneficial for all combinations of model and project. Overall 612 (96 unsupervised and 516 supervised) different project-model combinations[3] benefit from a WS larger than 1, additional 206 (37 unsupervised and 169 supervised) neither benefit nor take a loss, and only 414 (43 unsupervised and 371 supervised) report a decrease in the macro averaged F_1-score, which additionally take into account the size of both classes, so that not already a change in the distribution between the size of the faulty and non-faulty class can influence our result. Overall, approximated 33% of the model-project combinations are not improved by our

---

[3] For completeness, here, we also evaluated the possibility to use no Balancing or no Feature Compression technique. Those results are—as expected—weaker (cf. auxiliary material).

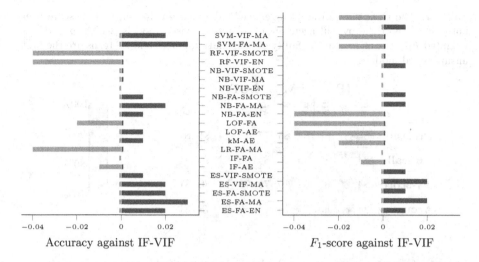

Fig. 7. Ten supervised models outperform the reference model IF-VIF (which scored 85% in all metrics) for the Eclipse project in terms of accuracy and F_1-score, but already five of them are variations of our ensemble model. Otherwise, only the NB model and some variations of SVMs are better models. Models, that are at least 3% worse in both measures than the IF-VIF model are omitted.

windowing technique, 50% do profit and about 17% are indifferent to the usage of a sliding window. Further analyses of our results show that the size of the last group shrinks with larger WS and more models either profit or not profit from the use of sliding windows. Also, as stated before, the quality decreases fast for larger WS, while the increase does not grow as fast as the decrease.

This effect can be caused by different aspects of the different datasets. Most of the models reporting a decrease in accuracy or F_1-score are evaluated with a project from the Unified GitHub dataset. For those projects, the sample size is very small and the share of faulty samples comparably great, since we can only evaluate on those files that are present in all revisions for consistency reasons, making the result dependent on only few samples. Also, in accordance with the no-free-lunch-theorem, a larger WS may simply be not suitable for the concrete model or set of metrics (e.g., static code metrics) [1].

It is desirable to evaluate models with a constant WS for comparability. We set our WS to 2, since—for this value—the decrease for the minority of models is relatively small, while the increase for the majority of models is almost as good as possible. In contrast, we have chosen variable WS for the Jureczko dataset to allow for the widest possible range of WS. This allows us to obtain additional validation for our findings, since we can test more WSs.

5.2 Outlier Models Compared to Other Cluster-Based Models

We investigate four different unsupervised algorithms (IF, LOF, kM, MS) with three different feature compression techniques (AE, FA, VIF). Table 2 shows that

Table 2. The table shows the average weighted Precision, Recall, and F_1-score over both classes and the overall accuracy of all unsupervised models, which exceeded a weighted F_1-score of 10% in the faulty class. Isolation Forest and k-Means are the best unsupervised models.

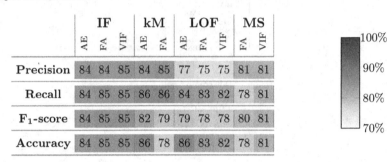

	IF			kM		LOF			MS	
	AE	FA	VIF	AE	FA	AE	FA	VIF	FA	VIF
Precision	84	84	85	84	85	77	75	75	81	81
Recall	84	85	85	86	86	84	83	82	78	81
F_1-score	84	85	85	82	79	79	78	78	80	81
Accuracy	84	85	85	86	78	86	83	82	78	81

100%
90%
80%
70%

from all of the unsupervised models the IF and the kM algorithm performed best. Unexpectedly, the IF with the VIF performed most consistent with a score of 85% followed closely by the IF with FA and kM with AE. In contrast to other unsupervised models, IF seem to actually prefer VIF as feature compression technique. Indeed, our evaluation reveals that in 10 out of 11 projects the IF performs better or is as good with VIF rather than FA in terms of accuracy and in 9 out of 11 projects in terms of the overall weighted F_1-score of both classes. So unlike previously mentioned by Kondo et al., IF as an unsupervised outlier mining model prefers a non-synthetic feature compression technique for most of the 11 projects [19]. Table 2 and our further evaluation (cf. auxiliary material) suggests that an IF with VIF is in the context of our computational experiment the best outlier mining algorithm and kM with AE or FA are the best cluster-based models. In Fig. 5, we further investigate those three models. The figure shows that indeed the IF with VIF is the top model among those models for our 11 example projects, achieving the best predicting scores for 10 out of 11 projects in terms of accuracy and 9 out of 11 projects in terms of the overall weighted F_1-score. Therefore, an IF is indeed a strong contender for unsupervised defect prediction, since they perform consistently over several projects.

5.3 Unsupervised vs. Supervised Models

Table 3 compares quality measures from all supervised models in addition to the IF with VIF for the Eclipse project. The best model is the ensemble of all supervised models (first three rows), outperforming the IF (next three rows) as consistent as possible on 11 out of 11 projects (Fig. 6). The IF performs not worse than any single supervised model. It is as good as one of the weaker supervised models. Although, single supervised model like a RF can outperform an IF quite consistently in 9 out of 11 interms of accuary and in 8 out of 11 cases in terms of the F_1-score. Figure 7 highlights that for the Eclipse project only a comparably small number of models can outperform our IF. As discussed in the previous

Table 3. The table shows that many supervised models outperform an IF. We evaluated our models using over both classes averaged weighted Precision, Recall, F_1-score, and overall Accuracy. The IF is still better than some models.

	ES (Ensemble)						IF (Iso. Forest)			LR (Logistic Regression)						
	FA-EN	FA-MA	FA-SMOTE	VIF-EN	VIF-MA	VIF-SMOTE	AE	FA	VIF	FA-EN	FA-MA	FA-SMOTE	VIF-EN	VIF-MA	VIF-SMOTE
Precision	86	87	86	87	87	87	84	84	85	87	88	87	87	87	87
Recall	87	88	87	78	87	86	84	85	85	79	80	78	78	78	78
F_1-score	86	87	86	81	87	86	84	85	85	82	83	80	81	81	81
Accuracy	87	88	87	78	87	86	84	85	85	79	80	78	78	78	78

100%
90%
80%
70%

	NB (Naive Bayes)						RF (Random Forest)						SVM (Sup. Vector Machine)					
	FA-EN	FA-MA	FA-SMOTE	VIF-EN	VIF-MA	VIF-SMOTE	FA-EN	FA-MA	FA-SMOTE	VIF-EN	VIF-MA	VIF-SMOTE	FA-EN	FA-MA	FA-SMOTE	VIF-EN	VIF-MA	VIF-SMOTE
Precision	86	85	86	86	87	86	86	87	86	87	87	87	86	86	86	85	85	85
Recall	86	87	86	85	85	85	79	78	80	81	76	81	75	88	75	80	87	80
F_1-score	86	86	86	85	86	85	81	81	82	83	79	83	78	86	78	82	83	82
Accuracy	86	87	86	85	85	85	79	78	80	81	76	81	75	88	75	80	87	80

section, the other unsupervised models can achieve a better result for this specific project and dataset in terms of accuracy, but fail to do this consistently on other projects or in terms of another metric like the F_1-score. As before, the ensembled model can achieve better results. It alone already represents half of the cases in which the IF was worse than a supervised model. Interestingly, for this project, no variation of the RF model can outperform our IF model, though here in place the NB model does so relatively consistently.

To summarize, the supervised models or at least the ensemble of supervised models show better results than an IF or any other unsupervised technique.

6   Discussion and Threats to Validity

We compared several basic models. Overall, outlier mining with IF with VIF has shown the best results among the unsupervised defect prediction techniques. However, several supervised models especially the ensemble of all supervised models seems to outperform any unsupervised technique. However, this effect is put into perspective by several additional requirements for training those models. On the one hand, we had to assume a history of recorded labels for the project, which is generally not the case in an industrial context [3,42]. Furthermore, we also favored supervised models by performing more preprocessing steps (class balancing, train-test-split, etc.), which are not required for unsupervised models. In addition, unsupervised models do not require a training phase. Therefore, we spent a significant amount of additional effort to train supervised models compared to unsupervised ones.

We premised several assumptions to make our sliding window technique applicable to our dataset. First, we have not distinguished whether there is one or more defects present in a given file. If a dataset reported more than one defect for the file, we assigned it the label for the faulty class. Second, the datasets reported a numerical label for a defect. Therefore, we could not track the case that a defect may be fixed inside of our window and another one is newly introduced. We only predict whether or not a defect is present in the file in the next revision of the software project. We set the random seed during our data processing to a constant value anywhere where randomness was involved. This, on the one hand, allows us to reproduce our results easily, but on the other hand raises the concern that we could only achieve those results for those specific seeds. However, we achieved our results analyzing several projects and since we did not optimize the seed for each project, it is very unlikely that this seed is especially beneficial for all our investigated projects. Usually, especially for supervised models one would use a random train-test split and a k-fold cross validation. However, here this step would increase the training time for our supervised models even further by the factor k, because also feature compression and class balancing would have to be repeated for each fold. This step would therefore undue favor our supervised models, since no training, and thus, no validation is required for unsupervised models. This is especially true since we already used a simple k-fold cross validation during optimization (only one iteration per hyperparameter set with 5 respectively 3 stratified folds).

In general, it is not possible to transfer results from one dataset to another due to the no-free-lunch theorem without restrictions [1]. Consequently, our results could be different on a different dataset or with different optimization techniques or, for example, different class balancing techniques. However, in the context of our computational experiment, it seems highly recommended to also seriously consider unsupervised techniques for defect prediction because we achieved our results from the evaluation of 11 projects and different sets of metrics. Here, the IF with VIF were also able to achieve a fairly consistent classification result. If the results of Bowes et al. can be extended to unsupervised techniques in future work, unsupervised techniques could also be used to reliably detect a certain class of defects [7]. Supervised models could subsequently specialize in those types of defects that are not so easily detectable by outlier mining techniques. In this way, a combination of supervised and unsupervised techniques could represent a simplification of previous methods, as already noted by Fu and Menzies [12].

We found some anomalies during our research. For example, as shown in Fig. 3, KM-FA did especially poorly for window size 8. As stated before, there is no guarantee that a model performing well on one dataset will perform as well on a similar but different dataset [1]. We suspect that this anomaly is an example of such an effect. Furthermore, most of our techniques maximized around 85% in any metric, which could be considered unacceptable for practical use. But, we purposefully concentrated on studying only basic models to get a basic overview of the performances of different methods so that a lower-than-usual quality can be expected.

In summary, it has been demonstrated that it can be beneficial to use unsupervised techniques, especially an IF, for defect prediction especially if no training labels are available and a fast prediction is desirable. This contrasts earlier results, which suggests that supervised techniques will usually outperform unsupervised techniques (cf. Huang et al. [16]).

7 Conclusions and Future Work

Using software metrics for defect prediction is widely used and typically viewed as a classification task, i.e., a supervised learning task. However, supervised learning techniques require a training dataset with training labels and require more (pre-) processing steps. Consequently, we proposed an approach using outlier mining techniques on time series of process metrics to reduce the processing steps.

The evaluation indicates that the proposed method is competitive to single basic supervised models. However, an ensemble of all basic supervised models outperforms any single unsupervised technique on all 11 projects. We still advocate the use of unsupervised models. Due to their ease of use and simplicity, they are more suitable as they require less development and execution time and no labels are required for training. In detail, the experiments are suggesting that an Isolation Forest with the Variance Inflation Factor used for feature compression is the most consistent option for predicting defects in an unsupervised fashion. However, other unsupervised models, e.g., the k-Means algorithm may perform better in certain cases.

Future research has to find a criterion to decide when which technique should be used to further improve an ensemble of models. We also suggest that further research should be conducted to investigate more complex unsupervised techniques for defect prediction, more preprocessing dimensions, and the explainability of models. Future research might also investigate more quality measures, e.g., the number of falsely reported files until the first hit when ordering the files according to their lines of code. In addition, a quantitative study evaluating our approach in an industrial setting may be beneficial.

Auxiliary Material. The auxiliary material to this paper is provided under: https://t1p.de/SoftwareQualityDays.

Acknowledgement. We thank the anonymous reviewers for their valuable feedback. This work was partially funded by the German Ministry for Education and Research (BMBF) through grants 01IS20088B ("KnowhowAnalyzer") and 01IS22062 ("AI research group FFS-AI").

References

1. Adam, S.P., Alexandropoulos, S.-A.N., Pardalos, P.M., Vrahatis, M.N.: No free lunch theorem: a review. In: Demetriou, I.C., Pardalos, P.M. (eds.) Approximation and Optimization. SOIA, vol. 145, pp. 57–82. Springer, Cham (2019). https://doi.org/10.1007/978-3-030-12767-1_5
2. Albahli, S.: A deep ensemble learning method for effort-aware just-in-time defect prediction. Future Internet 11(12), 246 (2019). https://doi.org/10.3390/fi11120246
3. Amasaki, S.: Cross-version defect prediction using cross-project defect prediction approaches: does it work? In: Proc. 14th International Conference on Predictive Models and Data Analytics in Software Engineering (PROMISE 2018), pp. 32–41. ACM (2018). https://doi.org/10.1145/3273934.3273938
4. Bennin, K.E., Keung, J., Monden, A., Kamei, Y., Ubayashi, N.: Investigating the effects of balanced training and testing datasets on effort-aware fault prediction models. In: Proc. 40th Annual Computer Software and Applications Conference (COMPSAC 2016), pp. 154–163. IEEE (2016). https://doi.org/10.1109/COMPSAC.2016.144
5. Bennin, K.E., Keung, J., Phannachitta, P., Monden, A., Mensah, S.: Mahakil: diversity based oversampling approach to alleviate the class imbalance issue in software defect prediction. IEEE Trans. Softw. Eng. 44(6), 534–550 (2018). https://doi.org/10.1109/TSE.2017.2731766
6. Bergstra, J., Bengio, Y.: Random search for hyper-parameter optimization. J. Mach. Learn. Res. 13(10), 281–305 (2012). https://jmlr.org/papers/v13/bergstra12a.html
7. Bowes, D., Hall, T., Gray, D.: Comparing the performance of fault prediction models which report multiple performance measures: recomputing the confusion matrix. In: Proc. 8th International Conference on Predictive Models in Software Engineering (PROMISE 2012), pp. 109–118. ACM (2012). https://doi.org/10.1145/2365324.2365338
8. Chawla, N.V., Bowyer, K.W., Hall, L.O., Kegelmeyer, W.P.: SMOTE: synthetic minority over-sampling technique. J. Artif. Intell. Res. 16(1), 321–357 (2002). https://doi.org/10.1613/jair.953
9. Chi, Y., Wang, H., Yu, P.S., Muntz, R.R.: Catch the moment: maintaining closed frequent itemsets over a data stream sliding window. Knowl. Inf. Syst. 10(3), 265–294 (2006). https://doi.org/10.1007/s10115-006-0003-0
10. Ding, Z., Fei, M.: An anomaly detection approach based on isolation forest algorithm for streaming data using sliding window. IFAC Proc. Vol. 46(20), 12–17 (2013). https://doi.org/10.3182/20130902-3-CN-3020.00044
11. Ferenc, R., Tóth, Z., Ladányi, G., Siket, I., Gyimóthy, T.: A public unified bug dataset for java. In: Proc. 14th International Conference on Predictive Models and Data Analytics in Software Engineering (PROMISE 2018), pp. 12–21. ACM (2018). https://doi.org/10.1145/3273934.3273936
12. Fu, W., Menzies, T.: Revisiting unsupervised learning for defect prediction. In: Proc. 11th Joint Meeting on Foundations of Software Engineering (ESEC/FSE 2017), pp. 72–83. ACM (2017). https://doi.org/10.1145/3106237.3106257
13. Hawkins, D.M.: The problem of overfitting. J. Chem. Inf. Comput. Sci. 44(1), 1–12 (2004). https://doi.org/10.1021/ci0342472
14. He, Z., Fan, B., Cheng, T., Wang, S.Y., Tan, C.H.: A mean-shift algorithm for large-scale planar maximal covering location problems. Eur. J. Oper. Res. 250(1), 65–76 (2016). https://doi.org/10.1016/j.ejor.2015.09.006

15. Hemmati, H., et al.: The MSR cookbook: mining a decade of research. In: Proc. 10th Working Conference on Mining Software Repositories (MSR 2013), pp. 343–352. IEEE (2013). https://doi.org/10.1109/MSR.2013.6624048

16. Huang, Q., Xia, X., Lo, D.: Supervised vs unsupervised models: a holistic look at effort-aware just-in-time defect prediction. In: Proc. International Conference on Software Maintenance and Evolution (ICSME 2017), pp. 159–170. IEEE (2017). https://doi.org/10.1109/ICSME.2017.51

17. Jiarpakdee, J., Tantithamthavorn, C., Hassan, A.E.: The impact of correlated metrics on the interpretation of defect models. IEEE Trans. Softw. Eng. **47**(2), 320–331 (2021). https://doi.org/10.1109/TSE.2019.2891758

18. Jureczko, M., Madeyski, L.: Towards identifying software project clusters with regard to defect prediction. In: Proc. 6th International Conference on Predictive Models in Software Engineering (PROMISE 2010). ACM (2010). https://doi.org/10.1145/1868328.1868342

19. Kondo, M., Bezemer, C.-P., Kamei, Y., Hassan, A.E., Mizuno, O.: The impact of feature reduction techniques on defect prediction models. Empir. Softw. Eng. **24**(4), 1925–1963 (2019). https://doi.org/10.1007/s10664-018-9679-5

20. Li, N., Shepperd, M., Guo, Y.: A systematic review of unsupervised learning techniques for software defect prediction. Inf. Softw. Technol. **122**, 106287 (2020). https://doi.org/10.1016/j.infsof.2020.106287

21. Li, Z., Jing, X.Y., Zhu, X.: Progress on approaches to software defect prediction. IET Softw. **12**(3), 161–175 (2018). https://doi.org/10.1049/iet-sen.2017.0148

22. Liu, F.T., Ting, K.M., Zhou, Z.H.: Isolation forest. In: Proc. 8th International Conference on Data Mining (ICDM 2008), pp. 413–422. IEEE (2008). https://doi.org/10.1109/ICDM.2008.17

23. Liu, Y., Li, Y., Guo, J., Zhou, Y., Xu, B.: Connecting software metrics across versions to predict defects. In: Proc. 25th International Conference on Software Analysis, Evolution and Reengineering (SANER 2018), pp. 232–243. IEEE (2018). https://doi.org/10.1109/SANER.2018.8330212

24. Mahmood, Z., Bowes, D., Lane, P.C.R., Hall, T.: What is the impact of imbalance on software defect prediction performance? In: Proc. 11th International Conference on Predictive Models and Data Analytics in Software Engineering (PROMISE 2015), pp. 1–4. ACM (2015). https://doi.org/10.1145/2810146.2810150

25. Mende, T.: Replication of defect prediction studies: problems, pitfalls and recommendations. In: Proc. 6th International Conference on Predictive Models in Software Engineering (PROMISE 2010), pp. 1–10. ACM (2010). https://doi.org/10.1145/1868328.1868336

26. Miles, J.: Tolerance and Variance Inflation Factor. Wiley (2014). https://doi.org/10.1002/9781118445112.stat06593

27. Moshtari, S., Santos, J.C., Mirakhorli, M., Okutan, A.: Looking for software defects? First find the nonconformists. In: Proc. 20th International Working Conference on Source Code Analysis and Manipulation (SCAM 2020), pp. 75–86. IEEE (2020). https://doi.org/10.1109/SCAM51674.2020.00014

28. Nagappan, N., Zeller, A., Zimmermann, T., Herzig, K., Murphy, B.: Change bursts as defect predictors. In: Proc. 21st International Symposium on Software Reliability Engineering (ISSRE 2010), pp. 309–318. IEEE (2010). https://doi.org/10.1109/ISSRE.2010.25

29. Nam, J., Kim, S.: CLAMI: defect prediction on unlabeled datasets. In: Proc. 30th IEEE/ACM International Conference on Automated Software Engineering (ASE 2015), pp. 452–463 (2015). https://doi.org/10.1109/ASE.2015.56

30. Powers, D.M.W.: Evaluation: from precision, recall and F-measure to ROC, informedness, markedness and correlation. J. Mach. Learn. Technol. **2**(1), 37–63 (2011)

31. Rathore, S.S., Kumar, S.: A study on software fault prediction techniques. Artif. Intell. Rev. **51**(2), 255–327 (2017). https://doi.org/10.1007/s10462-017-9563-5

32. Runeson, P.: A survey of unit testing practices. IEEE Softw. **23**(4), 22–29 (2006). https://doi.org/10.1109/MS.2006.91

33. Saravanan, R., Sujatha, P.: A state of art techniques on machine learning algorithms: a perspective of supervised learning approaches in data classification. In: 2018 Second International Conference on Intelligent Computing and Control Systems (ICICCS), pp. 945–949 (2018). https://doi.org/10.1109/ICCONS.2018.8663155

34. Sayyad Shirabad, J., Menzies, T.: The PROMISE repository of software engineering databases. School of Information Technology and Engineering, University of Ottawa, Canada (2005)

35. Tantithamthavorn, C., Hassan, A.E., Matsumoto, K.: The impact of class rebalancing techniques on the performance and interpretation of defect prediction models. IEEE Trans. Softw. Eng. **46**(11), 1200–1219 (2020). https://doi.org/10.1109/TSE.2018.2876537

36. Verleysen, M., François, D.: The curse of dimensionality in data mining and time series prediction. In: Cabestany, J., Prieto, A., Sandoval, F. (eds.) IWANN 2005. LNCS, vol. 3512, pp. 758–770. Springer, Heidelberg (2005). https://doi.org/10.1007/11494669_93

37. Xu, Z., et al.: Clustering-based unsupervised models, data analytics for defect prediction, empirical study. J. Syst. Softw. **172**, 110862 (2021). https://doi.org/10.1016/j.jss.2020.110862

38. Yan, M., Fang, Y., Lo, D., Xia, X., Zhang, X.: File-level defect prediction: unsupervised vs. supervised models. In: Proc. ACM/IEEE International Symposium on Empirical Software Engineering and Measurement (ESEM 2017), pp. 344–353. IEE/ACM (2017). https://doi.org/10.1109/ESEM.2017.48

39. Yang, Y., et al.: Effort-aware just-in-time defect prediction: simple unsupervised models could be better than supervised models. In: Proc. 24th ACM SIGSOFT International Symposium on Foundations of Software Engineering (FSE 2016), pp. 157–168. ACM (2016). https://doi.org/10.1145/2950290.2950353

40. Zhang, F., Zheng, Q., Zou, Y., Hassan, A.E.: Cross-project defect prediction using a connectivity-based unsupervised classifier. In: Proc. IEEE/ACM 38th International Conference on Software Engineering (ICSE 2016), pp. 309–320 (2016). https://doi.org/10.1145/2884781.2884839

41. Zhu, K., Zhang, N., Ying, S., Zhu, D.: Within-project and cross-project just-in-time defect prediction based on denoising autoencoder and convolutional neural network. IET Softw. **14**(3), 185–195 (2020). https://doi.org/10.1049/iet-sen.2019.0278

42. Zimmermann, T., Nagappan, N., Gall, H., Giger, E., Murphy, B.: Cross-project defect prediction: a large scale experiment on data vs. domain vs. process. In: Proc. 7th Joint Meeting of the European Software Engineering Conference and the ACM SIGSOFT Symposium on the Foundations of Software Engineering (ESEC/FSE 2009), pp. 91–100. ACM (2009). https://doi.org/10.1145/1595696.1595713

Software Testing

Applying a Genetic Algorithm for Test Suite Reduction in Industry

Philipp Stadler[1], Reinhold Plösch[1], and Rudolf Ramler[2](✉) (iD)

[1] Johannes Kepler University Linz, Linz, Austria
{philipp.stadler,reinhold.plosch}@jku.at
[2] Software Competence Center Hagenberg GmbH (SCCH), Hagenberg, Austria
rudolf.ramler@scch.at

Abstract. Time and cost of test execution increases when regression test suites grow over time. Techniques for test suite reduction have been proposed to streamline frequent test execution in continuous integration and to optimize the set of tests without sacrificing coverage and fault detection. In this paper we report on the design of a genetic algorithm to tackle the underlying optimization problem in context of an industry project from a software company developing tools for test automation. The prototypical implementation of the algorithm has been applied to the project's test suite containing several hundred test cases. We achieved an optimal solution with a 28% reduction of test cases. The evaluation of the reduced test suite using higher-level coverage and mutation analyses showed a minimal loss of coverage. The results demonstrated that the genetic algorithm can be successfully applied in industry and the achieved results are able to satisfy the requirements of the studied project. Nevertheless, major challenges have been identified by applying the approach in industry. They are related to the reliable collection of test execution data from previous test runs and dealing with test suites containing tests exhibiting unpredictable side-effects and flakiness.

Keywords: software testing · test suite optimization · test suite minimisation · genetic algorithm

1 Introduction

Whenever a software system is modified, bugs and unintended side-effects may be introduced. Regression testing is the process of re-testing the functionality of a new version of a software system by executing the test suite inherited from its previous version. The goal of this process is to ensure that the modifications made to a software system do not affect the existing, unchanged functionality [1].

Regression testing is a highly important quality assurance measure. However, it is also a time consuming and costly activity since a large part of the functionality of the software system has to be re-tested when a new version is released, even if only small changes have been made. Furthermore, the regression testing effort increases with every new software version that adds new functionality

© The Author(s), under exclusive license to Springer Nature Switzerland AG 2023
D. Mendez et al. (Eds.): SWQD 2023, LNBIP 472, pp. 63–83, 2023.
https://doi.org/10.1007/978-3-031-31488-9_4

and new tests to the regression test suite. This effect has been found to be particularly challenging with increasing emphasis on systematic reuse and shorter development cycles [2] as well as the introduction of continuous delivery [3] and continuous integration [4,5].

In reaction to the constantly increasing effort required for regression testing, a broad spectrum of methods has been proposed to optimize the regression tests [1]. The overall goal of these methods is to minimize the number of test cases that have to be executed in a regression test cycle. Typical approaches are reducing the regression test suite by removing redundant test cases [6], selecting a set of specific test cases from the full regression test suite for a test execution cycle [7], or by prioritising the test cases for execution so that faults are detected earlier in the regression test run [8].

The core of all of these approaches is an optimization problem. In this paper a genetic algorithm is proposed to tackle that problem in order to reduce the test cases of a regression test suite while preserving the coverage of the original test suite. Genetic algorithms have been found useful to solve a wide range of optimization problems, including regression test optimization (e.g., [9–12]). Our genetic algorithm for test suite reduction (Sect. 3) has been designed and implemented according to the requirements derived from a real-world industry project, which is described in Sect. 2. The proposed genetic algorithm was applied on the test suite of the industry project (Sect. 4). The resulting reduction of this test suite was evaluated using code coverage and mutation analysis (Sect. 5). The industry application demonstrated the feasibility and usefulness of the proposed approach. However, it also revealed a number of lessons learned about the obstacles we faced when performing test suite reduction in a real-world industry setting.

2 Research Approach

The **research objective** of the work reported in this paper is to *demonstrate the applicability of a test suite reduction approach using a genetic algorithm in industry*. Our research approach is based on the methodology and guidelines for design science by Wieringa [13]. In the following, we describe the industry context and the steps we conducted in order to achieve this objective.

2.1 Industry Context and Requirements

The software development project, where our genetic algorithm has been applied for test suite reduction, is developing the software tool *Devmate*[1]. It is the core product of our industry partner *Automated Software Testing GmbH*, a start-up company located in Austria.

Devmate is a testing tool designed to increase the efficiency of the software test automation process by means of combining AI and machine learning technologies for test case generation. The objective of applying our genetic algorithm

---

[1] https://www.devmate.software.

in context of this particular industry project has been twofold: First, the project maintains a comprehensive set comprising several hundred automated test cases that provides a suitable target for test suite reduction, which will help the project to streamline test execution in their continuous integration process. Second, the genetic algorithm designed for test suite reduction is also considered as a relevant approach to be possibly integrated in the tool itself, which is developed in the project.

Due to this context, following requirements for the application of the proposed genetic algorithm have been defined:

- *Test suite maintainability:* Test suite reduction is often associated with the reduction of test execution time. In our case, however, the main consideration was the maintainability of the test suite. The tool Devmate is specialised in the automatic generation of test cases. The introduction of duplicated or unnecessary test cases into a test suite should therefore be avoided in order to keep the maintainability high. Thus, the genetic algorithm should be able to reduce the number of test cases in a test suite without significantly lowering the statement coverage.
- *Language independent:* The tool Devmate is developed in Java and the test cases are also implemented in the Java programming language. However, the genetic algorithm and the prototype implementation had to be designed to be independent from the specifics of a particular programming language or technology, so they remain applicable to test suites using multiple programming languages from which test execution histories can be recorded.
- *Tool independent:* The genetic algorithm design should not rely on the test execution histories provided by a specific coverage tool or format. Our test suite reduction approach relies on test execution histories that are recorded by using existing code coverage tools. Since such coverage tools are typically developed and optimized for a specific programming language, it must be ensured that the genetic algorithm is applicable to the test execution histories produced by different coverage tools.
- *Modular application:* The genetic algorithm should be able to reduce the test cases of a test suite entirely as well as partially to maintain flexibility about future application scenarios. The different possible needs regarding the granularity of test suite reduction range from the reduction of all of a test suite's test cases, to the reduction of a test suite's test cases from specific packages, classes or even from individual methods. This requirement implies scalability to test suites with a large number of test cases and, at the same time, to test suites with only a few test cases. Test suite reduction should provide meaningful results in both cases.
- *Fast results:* Test suite reduction is a complex optimization problem that typically requires a significant overhead for producing optimal solutions on large test suites with highly interdependent test cases [14,15]. In order to support integration in the tool Devmate, however, the genetic algorithm is required to produce fast results for selecting test cases to be excluded from generated test suites while maintaining the same level of coverage.

2.2   Development and Evaluation Procedure

Overall, the development and evaluation procedure comprises 5 steps in order to achieve our research objective. First, the industry context and requirements are defined as necessary basis for our work. Then, the genetic algorithm is designed and implemented. In the last two steps, the proposed approach is applied and evaluated in context of the selected industry project. Figure 1 provides an overview of these steps, which are described in detail below.

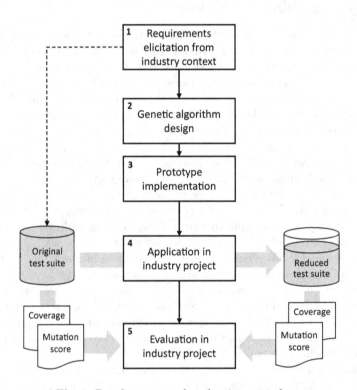

Fig. 1. Development and evaluation procedure

1. **Requirements elicitation from industry context.** Together with our industry partner we defined requirements and success criteria for test suite reduction. Furthermore, a real-world project has been selected for applying the proposed approach. This project provided a suite of automated test cases as basis for evaluating the optimization results. Besides more general goals mentioned above, the core goal of this work is to reduce the number of test cases in a way that the original coverage can mostly be achieved.
2. **Design of a genetic algorithm** that can be used to optimize an existing test suite (i.e., reduce redundant test cases) based on coverage information.

In our design, we followed the basic principles and recommendations for genetic algorithms suggested by related work.

3. **Prototype implementation.** A prototype tool for test suite reduction using the designed genetic algorithm was developed in Python. It uses test execution data collected from our industry partner's project as input and produces a suggestion for an optimized test suite as output.

4. **Application in industry project.** Test execution data was collected with the open source coverage tool OpenClover[2] and converted into a format processable by our prototype. The result, i.e., the proposed reduction of test cases, was subsequently applied to the existing test suite, a snapshot of the test suite from the Devmate project.

5. **Evaluation in industry project.** For evaluating the proposed test suite reduction approach in context of a real-world industry project, coverage and mutation measurements were taken from the reduced test suite and compared to the data from the original test suite to identify any differences. We applied a different coverage tool (JaCoCo[3]) and, in addition, mutation testing with PIT[4] to obtain independent measurements. Furthermore, organizational challenges and technical obstacles recorded throughout the entire process were used as basis for a qualitative evaluation.

3 Genetic Algorithm Design

In this section we describe the design of the genetic algorithm used for optimizing an existing test suite. It relies on information about past test executions. These *test histories* are basically the execution traces of the test cases, representing the information about which line, statement, or branch is covered by which test.

Table 1 shows the test histories comprising information of covered statements of 5 test cases. The test execution information is necessary for the coverage determination of a given test suite respectively the fitness calculation of a given chromosome. For example, a test suite TS_1 containing test case tc_4 has a lower fitness than a test suite TS_2 containing test case tc_5, since only 9 instead of 15 statements out of a total of 16 statements are covered by 1 test case.

3.1 Population

The first step of the design of our genetic algorithm concerns the initialization of the population, i.e. a number of arbitrary test suites. These test suites are represented by binary arrays. They are generated from the set of available test cases by randomly selecting which test cases will be executed in which test suite. An exemplary population based on the test cases of Table 1 is shown in Table 2.

---

[2] https://openclover.org/.

[3] https://www.jacoco.org.

[4] https://pitest.org.

Table 1. Test histories

Statement	Test case				
	tc_1	tc_2	tc_3	tc_4	tc_5
S_1	x	x	x	x	x
S_2	x	x	x	x	x
S_3	x	x	x	x	x
S_4	x	x	x	x	x
S_5	x	x	x	x	x
S_6			x		x
S_7			x		x
S_8			x		x
S_9	x	x	x	x	x
S_{10}	x	x	x	x	x
S_{11}	x			x	x
S_{12}		x	x		
S_{13}	x	x	x	x	x
S_{14}			x		x
S_{15}			x		x
S_{16}			x		x

Table 2. Population with its binary representation of test suites

Chromosome/test suite	Gene/test case tc_i				
	1	2	3	4	5
TS_1	0	0	0	0	1
TS_2	0	0	0	1	0
TS_3	1	1	0	0	0
TS_4	1	1	1	1	1
TS_5	1	1	0	1	1

The binary values of the arrays indicate whether a test case will be executed or not. For example, only the gene tc_5 of the chromosome TS_1 was set to 1, which means that the test suite TS_1 only contains test case tc_5 for execution.

3.2   Fitness Calculation

In the second step, the chromosomes of the generated population are evaluated. Therefore a fitness function representing the optimization problem is defined, which is then used to evaluate every chromosome of the population.

The optimisation problem at hand is to find a test suite that maximises coverage and minimises the amount of test case executions. The second part of the optimisation, i.e. the amount of test case executions, can be determined on the basis of the binary representations of each test suite (see Table 2) by summing up the genes. For the first part of the optimisation, i.e. the coverage of a test suite, the test histories of the included test cases are combined to a binary representation. Table 3 shows such a combined binary representation based on the population from Table 2 and the test histories from Table 1.

Table 3. Binary representation of the combined test histories

Chromosome/test suite	Covered statement S_i															
	1	2	3	4	5	6	7	8	9	10	11	12	13	14	15	16
TS_1	1	1	1	1	1	1	1	1	1	1	1	0	1	1	1	1
TS_2	1	1	1	1	1	0	0	0	1	1	1	0	1	0	0	0
TS_3	1	1	1	1	1	0	0	0	1	1	1	1	1	0	0	0
TS_4	1	1	1	1	1	1	1	1	1	1	1	1	1	1	1	1
TS_5	1	1	1	1	1	1	1	1	1	1	1	1	1	1	1	1

The binary values of the cells indicate whether a statement is covered by the test cases of a test suite or not. The coverage of a test suite can therefore be calculated by summing up the binary values and dividing them by the number of total statements. For example, test suite TS_4 and test suite TS_5 have a coverage of 100 percent, since all statements are covered.

These fitness values are used to determine the fittest chromosome of a population by ranking the chromosomes according to our definition of the optimisation problem (see Table 4).

3.3 Fittest Chromosome

The third step of the genetic algorithm design provides that the present fittest chromosome, i.e. the fittest chromosome within a population, is compared to the overall fittest chromosome, i.e. the fittest chromosome across all populations.

According to our definition of the optimisation problem, the fittest chromosome is the test suite that maximises coverage and minimises the amount of test case executions. When we evaluate the fitness values in Table 4, the test suite TS_5 is the present fittest chromosome, because it achieves the highest coverage with the lowest number of test cases.

Table 4. Determination of the fittest chromosome

Chromosome/test suite	Number of genes/test cases	Coverage of statements
TS_5	4	100%
TS_4	5	100%
TS_1	1	94%
TS_3	2	62%
TS_2	1	56%

After determining the present fittest chromosome C_P, a comparison with the overall fittest chromosome C_O is performed. First, it is evaluated whether C_P has a greater coverage than C_O. If this is the case, C_P becomes the new overall fittest chromosome. If the coverage of the two chromosomes is the same, then the number of test cases is compared. If C_P has fewer test cases than C_O, C_P becomes the new overall fittest chromosome. In all other cases C_O remains unchanged, i.e. in those cases where the C_P achieves smaller coverage or comprises a larger number of test cases than C_O.

Note that the comparison between C_P and C_O can only be performed after the first iteration of running the genetic algorithm, since no overall fittest chromosome exists in the first iteration.

3.4   Biologically Inspired Operations

In the fifth step, the biologically inspired operations *selection*, *crossover* and *mutation* are applied to the current population for generating a new population. These operations are executed several times and in sequence on the current population's chromosomes. The result of a single execution is a new chromosome that is added to the new population.

To generate a new chromosome, a *selection operation* is first applied to the current population. This selection operation selects two random chromosomes, also called parents, whereby the selection of parents is not purely by chance. Instead, a specific bias is introduced so that fitter chromosomes are preferred in the selection process. This ensures that the fitness of the new population increases with high probability, which means that the chance of finding fitter chromosomes increases. For example, the so-called tournament selection represents such a method. In this method, the selection is done by comparing the fitness of an arbitrary number of chromosomes derived from the current population. The fittest chromosome found in this comparison becomes one parent and the same process is repeated to select the second parent. Other selection methods [16,17] are, for example, the roulette wheel selection, rank selection, or stochastic universal sampling.

After the parents have been selected, a *crossover operation* is applied. It generates a new chromosome, also called child, by mixing the genes of the parents. The mixing depends on the chosen method of crossover. For example, the single-point crossover is a method that splits the genes of the parents at a randomly selected point. The result are two gene segments per parent, where one of these segments is swapped with each other. Other crossover methods [16,17] are, for example, the multi-point crossover or the uniform crossover.

Before the child is finally added to the new population, a *mutation operation* is applied. A mutation operation basically alters one or more of the child's genes to generate a new chromosome, which is called mutant. This is done to cover the available search space more effectively. Since our genetic algorithm works with binary representations of test suites, it is sufficient to flip one or more randomly chosen binary values of the child's genes.

Table 5 shows an exemplary application of a single-point crossover and a bit-flip mutation. The selected parents are the test suites TS_3 and TS_5 from Table 2.

Table 5. Selection, crossover and mutation

Selection	Gene/test case tc_i				
	1	2	3	4	5
TS_3	1	1	0	0	0
TS_5	1	1	0	1	1
Crossover	TS_3 gene segment 1			TS_5 gene segment 2	
Child	1	1	0	1	1
Mutation	TS_3 gene segment 1			Bit-Flip	
Mutant	1	1	0	1	0

The biologically inspired operations are executed several times to create a new population with the same number of chromosomes as the current population. It consists of mutants, generated chromosomes from the crossover operation (i.e. children), as well as chromosomes from the current population. The proportion of mutants, children and current chromosomes in the new population is defined by the so-called crossover threshold and the mutation probability.

The crossover threshold defines the proportion of the current chromosomes (survivors) and newly generated chromosomes in the new population. For example, a threshold of 75% means that the new population consists of 25% survivors and 75% newly generated chromosomes. The mutation probability, on the other hand, defines the probability of whether a chromosome generated by the crossover operation will be mutated by the mutation operation or not. This means that the newly generated chromosomes can be either children or mutants. Typically the mutation probability is rather low so that the genetic algorithm does not get reduced to a random search. However, mutation is necessary to introduce and maintain diversity in the new population.

3.5   Evolution and Termination

With the new population at hand all steps beginning with the fitness calculation are repeated until a termination condition is reached. A termination condition can be the continuity of an overall fittest chromosome or the exceeding of a certain evolution. How the termination condition is chosen depends to a large extent on the optimisation problem being solved and on the parameters of the algorithm, i.e., population size, crossover threshold, and mutation probability.

The result of the proposed genetic algorithm is the overall fittest chromosome found. This chromosome represents a test suite which maximises statement coverage and minimises the amount of test case executions. Table 6 shows three possible test suites, which have been generated by multiple runs based on the test histories of Table 1.

Table 6. Results

Test suite	Test cases	Covered statements
$Result_1$	tc_3, tc_5	$S_1, S_2, S_3, S_4, S_5, S_6, S_7, S_8, S_9, S_{10}, S_{11}, S_{12}, S_{13}, S_{14}, S_{15}, S_{16}$
$Result_2$	tc_3, tc_4	$S_1, S_2, S_3, S_4, S_5, S_6, S_7, S_8, S_9, S_{10}, S_{11}, S_{12}, S_{13}, S_{14}, S_{15}, S_{16}$
$Result_3$	tc_2, tc_5	$S_1, S_2, S_3, S_4, S_5, S_6, S_7, S_8, S_9, S_{10}, S_{11}, S_{12}, S_{13}, S_{14}, S_{15}, S_{16}$

The reason why the proposed genetic algorithm generates different results over various runs is mainly due to the small size of the given optimisation problem and the used fitness calculation that only considers statement coverage and the number of test case executions. However, it has the advantage that the fitness calculation can easily be extended respectively adapted, for example, by considering the execution time or the priority of the test cases.

4   Industry Application

A prototype of the designed genetic algorithm was developed in Python and applied in a real-world project of our industry partner. First, the test execution histories were collected with an open source coverage tool, namely OpenClover, and converted into the JSON format processable by our prototype. The result, i.e., the proposed reduction of test cases, was subsequently applied to the existing test suite. In addition, coverage measures from another coverage tool (JaCoco) and from mutation testing (based on PIT), were used to evaluate the quality of the test suite reduction.

4.1   Original Test Suite

The test suite from our industry project consisted of a total of 389 test cases. Overall, this test suite reached a coverage of 68.3%. of the source code, measured with the tool OpenClover. The coverage measurement shows that 20 out of 34 source code packages were covered. OpenClover calculates only a single coverage value per package, which is a combination of statement and branch coverage, considering the number of methods entered.

A problem was encountered during collecting measurement data from mutation testing. Some of the code exercised by the test cases accessed the file system to read or write documents. Since mutation testing involves injecting mutants, i.e. potentially faulty changes into the code, the execution of the test suite was prohibited by the mutation testing tool PIT in order to protect the file system from corrupting changes. To solve this problem, we had to remove 143 test cases from the test suite. After removing the problematic test cases with file access, the adjusted test suite contained 246 test cases. This test suite achieved a code coverage of 57% and an average mutation score of 52%.

Table 7 lists the detailed measurement results for the packages P_1 to P_{34}. The column *OpenClover* shows the reported combined coverage values and the number of executed test cases per package. (Note: A test case is associated to every package covered by this test, i.e., individual test cases may be counted several times in the column Tests.) The tool *JaCoCo* allows to measure coverage values for statement and branch coverage individually. The measurements from PIT are divided into the columns injected mutants, killed mutants, and coverage. Injected mutants represents the number of modifications introduced in the source code and killed mutants represents the number of modifications, which were detected by the executed test cases. Finally, the column coverage contains the reported mutation coverage according to PIT.

It has to be noted that JaCoCo as well as PIT report *NaN* as result for 3 packages. The reason is that some of the packages are located in different modules and no coverage is reported by JaCoCo and PIT for packages of a module with no test cases. OpenClover, however, aggregates the coverage data from modules and therefore the coverage is reported for the affected packages as they are tested based on another module's test cases.

4.2   Test Suite Reduction Using Genetic Algorithm

The genetic algorithm was applied to the recorded test execution histories with following parameter settings: a population size of 20, a crossover threshold of 0.65 using a rank selection and uniform crossover, a mutation probability of 0.35 using a bit-flip mutation, and a termination condition of 200 evolutions. These parameter settings showed the most promising results across several applications.

We repeated the application of the genetic algorithm with these settings multiple times to obtain a range of results for our evaluation. The different values obtained from individual runs are an effect of the randomness of the genetic algorithm, even when these runs are executed with the exact same parameter settings. The results from five different applications are shown in Table 8.

The multiple applications of the proposed genetic algorithm achieved an average reduction of 67.6 test cases, which corresponds to an average reduction of the test suite to 72.5% of it's original size.

The best reduction was achieved by genetic algorithm application A_4 with 74 reduced test cases, compared to application A_3 with only 63 reduced test cases. The average execution time of the genetic algorithm needed to compute the optimization was 139.8 s. The execution time differences between the five runs are marginal.

Table 7. Coverage measurements from the original test suite

Package	OpenClover		JaCoCo		PIT		
	Coverage	Tests	Statement	Branch	Injected	Killed	Coverage
P_1	100%	100	NaN	NaN	NaN	NaN	NaN
P_2	100%	7	100%	100%	11	11	100%
P_3	98%	114	97%	100%	32	28	88%
P_4	97%	140	NaN	NaN	NaN	NaN	NaN
P_5	91%	55	91%	67%	99	40	40%
P_6	90%	64	96%	83%	14	12	86%
P_7	81%	7	85%	70%	19	16	84%
P_8	81%	21	88%	75%	8	0	0%
P_9	77%	160	63%	35%	159	72	45%
P_{10}	75%	148	NaN	NaN	NaN	NaN	NaN
P_{11}	73%	120	70%	58%	104	60	58%
P_{12}	65%	10	64%	50%	31	19	61%
P_{13}	65%	24	69%	63%	98	73	74%
P_{14}	60%	113	42%	18%	391	113	29%
P_{15}	43%	41	31%	44%	21	11	52%
P_{16}	37%	103	39%	16%	42	8	19%
P_{17}	35%	8	45%	0%	7	3	43%
P_{18}	34%	59	26%	33%	22	8	36%
P_{19}	13%	4	12%	30%	23	3	13%
P_{20}	0%	0	63%	63%	321	172	54%
P_{21}	0%	0	0%	0%	669	0	0%
P_{22}	0%	0	0%	0%	602	0	0%
P_{23}	0%	0	0%	0%	582	0	0%
P_{24}	0%	0	0%	0%	551	0	0%
P_{25}	0%	0	0%	0%	48	0	0%
P_{26}	0%	0	0%	0%	33	0	0%
P_{27}	0%	0	0%	0%	16	0	0%
P_{28}	0%	0	0%	0%	13	0	0%
P_{29}	0%	0	0%	0%	4	0	0%
P_{30}	0%	0	0%	0%	0	0	0%
P_{31}	0%	0	0%	0%	0	0	0%
P_{32}	0%	0	0%	0%	0	0	0%
P_{33}	0%	0	0%	0%	0	0	0%
P_{34}	0%	0	0%	0%	0	0	0%

Table 8. Results of the genetic algorithm applications

Application	Number of reduced tests	Reduced test suite size	Algorithm execution
A_1	−66	73.2 %	139 s
A_2	−68	72.4 %	138 s
A_3	−63	74.4 %	142 s
A_4	−74	69.9 %	141 s
A_5	−67	72.8 %	139 s

4.3 Reduced Test Suite

The genetic algorithm application run A_2 from Table 8 is the one closest to the average reduction. We applied the results from this run to reduce the test suite for further evaluation.

The output of a genetic algorithm application is a list of test cases, indicating for each of them whether it should be kept or whether it can be removed from the existing test suite. According to the genetic algorithm application A_2, 68 test cases can be safely removed from the existing test suite without reducing code coverage according to the measurement performed with OpenClover. Furthermore, in order to evaluate the reduced test suite and the possible influence of the used covereage tool, the coverage measurement and mutation analysis were repeated on the reduced test suite with JaCoCo and PIT.

Table 9 shows the measurement results obtained for the packages P_1 to P_{20}, i.e. only the packages that exhibited a coverage in the existing test suite. Overall, the reduced test suite achieved a total coverage of 56.9% with only 178 tests executed. This corresponds to an overall coverage loss of 0.1% with a 28% reduction of test case executions. Regarding the average mutation coverage, a loss of 1% was observed, i.e. the test suite has an average mutation coverage of 51%.

5 Evaluation and Discussion

In this section we analyze the achieved reduction of test cases based on the coverage measurements provided by *OpenClover*, which we then compare to the coverage measurements from *JaCoCo* and the mutation score from *PIT*. Finally, we discuss our observations and the lessons learned from the application in context of the industry project.

5.1 Reduction of Test Cases

As basis for our evaluation of the achieved results, the measurements from the original test suite were subtracted from the of the reduced test suite. Table 10 provides an overview of the computed differences per package.

From the measurement differences for *OpenClover* one can observe that a reduction of test case was achieved for all packages (except for package P_{20},

Table 9. Coverage measurements from the reduced test suite

Package	OpenClover		JaCoCo		PIT		
	Coverage	Tests	Statement	Branch	Injected	Killed	Coverage
P_1	100%	90	NaN	NaN	NaN	NaN	NaN
P_2	88%	2	98%	58%	11	10	91%
P_3	97%	82	97%	100%	32	28	88%
P_4	97%	123	NaN	NaN	NaN	NaN	NaN
P_5	91%	46	91%	67%	99	39	39%
P_6	90%	49	96%	83%	14	12	86%
P_7	81%	5	85%	70%	19	16	84%
P_8	81%	16	88%	75%	8	0	0%
P_9	77%	133	63%	35%	159	72	45%
P_{10}	75%	129	NaN	NaN	NaN	NaN	NaN
P_{11}	73%	101	70%	58%	104	60	58%
P_{12}	65%	7	64%	46%	31	18	58%
P_{13}	64%	21	68%	59%	98	71	72%
P_{14}	60%	98	42%	18%	391	113	29%
P_{15}	43%	32	31%	44%	21	11	52%
P_{16}	37%	89	39%	16%	42	8	19%
P_{17}	35%	7	45%	0%	7	3	43%
P_{18}	34%	54	26%	33%	22	8	36%
P_{19}	13%	3	12%	20%	23	2	9%
P_{20}	0%	0	63%	63%	321	143	45%

which did not contain any associated test cases in the original test suite). For most packages, a significant number of associated tests could be reduced. For example, up to –32 for package P_3, which is a reduction of 28%. The average reduction is -10.55 tests per package (median –9). Despite this reduction, the coverage of the original test suite was preserved for all packages except one.

For package P_2 a coverage loss of 12% was recorded. The reason is that the coverage values reported by OpenClover are a combination of statement coverage and branch coverage, while only statement coverage has been considered as basis for the optimization by our genetic algorithm. The code in package P_2 contains two *if* statements without *else* branches, for which the corresponding test cases were missed in the optimization process.

5.2 Coverage and Mutation Analysis

For a more detailed evaluation, we also used *JaCoCo* to record statement and branch coverage. These measurements show a loss of statement coverage of –2% at package P_2 and –1% at package P_{13} as well as a loss in branch coverage of

Table 10. Measurement differences

Package	OpenClover		JaCoCo		PIT		
	Coverage	Tests	Statement	Branch	Injected	Killed	Coverage
P_1	0%	−10	NaN	NaN	NaN	NaN	NaN
P_2	−12%	−5	−2%	−42%	0	−1	−9%
P_3	0%	−32	0%	0%	0	0	0%
P_4	0%	−17	NaN	NaN	NaN	NaN	NaN
P_5	0%	−9	0%	0%	0	−1	−1%
P_6	0%	−15	0%	0%	0	0	0%
P_7	0%	−2	0%	0%	0	0	0%
P_8	0%	−5	0%	0%	0	0	0%
P_9	0%	−27	0%	0%	0	0	0%
P_{10}	0%	−19	NaN	NaN	NaN	NaN	NaN
P_{11}	0%	−19	0%	0%	0	0	0%
P_{12}	0%	−3	0%	−4%	0	−1	−3%
P_{13}	0%	−3	−1%	−4%	0	−2	−2%
P_{14}	0%	−15	0%	0%	0	0	0%
P_{15}	0%	−9	0%	0%	0	0	0%
P_{16}	0%	−14	0%	0%	0	0	0%
P_{17}	0%	−1	0%	0%	0	0	0%
P_{18}	0%	−5	0%	0%	0	0	0%
P_{19}	0%	−1	0%	−10%	0	−1	−4%
P_{20}	0%	0	0%	0%	0	−29	−9%

up to –42% at package P_2. A loss in branch coverage is also shown at package P_{12} and P_{19}, for which statement coverage has been preserved. These the differences in the measurements are a result of JaCoCo analyzing coverage differently than OpenClover[5] and at a more detailed level, including conditional statements containing combined conditions[6].

The evaluation using *PIT* for mutation analysis shows similar results. A loss in mutation coverage has been found in packages that already exhibited a loss in branch coverage (P_2, P_{12}, P_{13} and P_{19}) as well as in two other packages (P_5 and P_{20}). The majority of the surviving mutants are associated to package P_{20}. These mutants survived because OpenClover did not associate any test cases to this package (see Table 7) and, thus, no test execution histories were available for the correct optimization by the genetic algorithm.

---

[5] https://stackoverflow.com/questions/24369631/clover-and-jacoco-give-different-code-coverage-results.

[6] https://stackoverflow.com/questions/63492529/why-is-jacoco-coverage-report-for-branches-saying-if-a-b-c-is-actually-6.

Table 11. Surviving mutants by mutation operator and package

Package	Mutation operator			Sum
	Return values	Negate conditionals	Void method call	
P_2	1			1
P_5	1			1
P_{12}	1			1
P_{13}	1	1		2
P_{19}		1		1
P_{20}		3	26	29
Sum	4	5	26	35

Overall, a total of 35 mutants survived due to the reduction of test cases. These mutants can be traced back to four different mutators, which are mutation operations changing specific aspects of the program under test. Table 11 shows the surviving mutants by mutator and source code package. We performed a detailed analysis of the source code locations containing survived mutants which provided following insights.

– The mutator *void method call* caused 26 of the survived mutants. This mutation operation removes calls to *void* methods. Affected code locations contained calls to methods of the class *StringConcatenation*, which were all located in package P_{20} neglected by in the optimization process.
– Another 5 mutants were caused by the mutator *negate conditionals*, a mutation operation that substitutes conditionals to their negated counterparts. This operation affected conditional cases of several *if* statements in package P_{20} as well as *if* statements in P_{13} and P_{19} using combined conditions (i.e., condition including the logical operator *OR*). They were missed in the optimisation process due to the insufficient level of detail in the coverage measures provided by OpenClover.
– The remaining 4 were introduced by the mutator *return values* in the packages P_2, P_5, P_{12} and P_{13}. This mutation operation changes the return values of methods depending on their return type. For example, return values of type *boolean* are changed to *true* or *false*, *string* and *collection* are changed to empty strings and empty collections, *primitives* (*int*, *char*, etc.) are changed to *0*, and other return values are simply set to *null*. The affected code locations were three *getter* methods and a *lambda* expression for filtering a collection. The mutants survived because the affected statements were called from the tested method but their coverage was not associated with the source package, which is why it was not considered in the optimization by the genetic algorithm. These mutants can be avoided by revising the optimization approach to also consider indirectly coverage, i.e., covered code residing outside the tested package.

5.3   Observations and Lessons Learned

We encountered several issues and obstacles when we applied the proposed genetic algorithm for test suite reduction in the industry project. Most of them are not a consequence of using a genetic algorithm to address the underlying optimization problem. They are technical issues related to the implementation of the test cases in the project's regression test suite as well as specific issues introduced by the tools used for collecting coverage data and test execution histories.

In the following we discuss these issues and their consequences for applying test suite reduction in practice. Furthermore, we also provide insights and general lessons learned from designing and implementing our approach according to the requirements from industry.

Successful Reduction of Test Cases. First of all, the successful reduction of test cases from the project's regression test suit has to be emphasized. As shown in the previous section, the proposed genetic algorithm was able to reduce the size of the provided test suite without significantly affecting the coverage measure used in the optimization process. Overall, 68 test cases were removed with a marginal coverage loss of 0.1%. The size of reduction relates to a noticeable speed-up in test execution in the industry project, where the tests are frequently run as part of the continuous integration cycle.

Improving Efficiency over Effectiveness. Related research on regression test optimization emphasizes the goal of safe regression testing [18,19] that aims to prevents any loss of coverage. In contrast, our industry application showed that in practice some loss of coverage and even a marginal reduction of the ability to find all bugs is acceptable. As long as the full regression test suite is still executed from time to time, no bugs will be missed in the final, released version of the software system. This can be achieved by using the optimized test suite, for example, in continuous integration to speed up test execution and by periodically running the entire test suite in nightly builds. The trade-off between improving efficiency and effectiveness is also discussed in [20], where the authors point out that test suit reduction should not result in a permanent removal of test cases from the regression test suite.

Time Requirements for Optimization. While our approach using a genetic algorithm was able to provide significant and practically relevant optimization results, it turned out that – based on our prototypical implementation – the run-time of the optimization does not fulfill our initially defined requirements. In order to provide an improvement in terms of efficiency, the time required for the optimization process and the execution of the reduced test suite should be less than running the original test suite. The average execution time of the genetic algorithm needed to compute the optimization was 139.8 s (see Table 8), which is more than the execution time of the original test suite. Thus, our suggestion is to run the optimization only occasionally, e.g., when major changes of the test suite or the system under test have been made. Furthermore, there is still potential to optimize the implementation of the genetic algorithm, in particular by following an incremental optimization process [21] where the initialisation of the population is based on previous optimal solutions.

Pitfalls of Mutation Analysis. Mutation analysis was used in the evaluation of the proposed approach. In this process we encountered the issues that the code exercised by some of the test cases accessed the file system to read and write documents. Mutating this code was prohibited by the tool PIT in order to prevent corrupting changes made to the file system. As a consequence, we were not able to include the associated test cases in our evaluation. 143 test cases were excluded and the evaluation was finally performed with an adjusted test suite. From the perspective of the proposed optimization approach, this step would not have been necessary since there were no limitations in collecting coverage data from all tests including those we had to exclude. However, the described issue affected the evaluation of our work.

Difficulties in Obtaining Reliable Coverage Measurements. In our work we used three different tools for measuring code and mutation coverage. Open-Clover, a freely available open source tool, was used to collect information about test execution histories that are the basis for our genetic algorithm. JaCoCo, another open source coverage tool, was used in our evaluation as a control instance to verify the coverage reported by OpenClover. The mutation testing tool PIT was used in the evaluation to determine the quality of the reduced test suite. Besides the issues described above regarding the use of PIT on code that accesses the file system, we also encountered the problem that JaCoCo as well as PIT did not report coverage values for three packages (NaN entries in Table 7), since coverage measures are not aggregated to packages in the same way as by OpenClover. On the other hand, OpenClover did not record any data for one of the packages while JaCoCo did. The reason is still under investigation. Users have to be aware that such issues caused by missing data can have a severe impact on the genetic algorithm's ability to completely and reliably optimise the existing test suite.

Tool-Dependent Coverage Measurement Differences. Our evaluation using different coverage tools also revealed that different coverage measurement values are reported by different tools for the same tests. Even when we neglect the issue that one tool does not provide measurements for a specific package although the other does, and vice versa, the coverage measurements provided by both tools are not comparable. These discrepancies have several reasons. One reason is the specific way how each tool reports coverage measures, e.g., Open-Clover reports a combination of statement and branch coverage and considers the number of methods entered. Another reason are differences in how coverage is measured, e.g., JaCoCo distinguishes conditional statements considering also individual conditions combined by logical operators. Hence, although both tools report branch coverage, these sometimes subtle and hard to notice differences cause discrepancies that ultimately result in a coverage loss in the optimization process (see Table 10). Nevertheless, irregularities between the measurement results of different coverage tools are also reported in the literature [22,23] and approaches relying on coverage measurements have to be implemented in a tool-agnostic way. Our implementation, for example, uses a tool-independent format for coverage data as input for the genetic algorithm. So even if the coverage tool changes due to a different programming language or due to the availability of another tool or a new version, performing test suite reductions is still possible with the proposed genetic algorithm.

6 Summary

In this paper we presented an approach for regression test suite reduction based on a genetic algorithm. We designed the genetic algorithm to tackle the underlying optimization problem according to the requirements derived from a real-world industry project of a software company developing tools for test automation. The prototypical implementation of the algorithm has been applied to the project's test suite containing several hundred test cases. It successfully achieved an optimal solution with a 28% reduction of test cases. A total of 68 test cases were removed from the original test suite.

The evaluation of the reduced test suite using additional coverage and mutation analyses showed a marginal loss of coverage: an overall coverage loss of 0.1% and an average mutation coverage loss of 1%. These results demonstrate that the genetic algorithm can be successfully applied in industry and the achieved results are able to satisfy the requirements of the studied project. Nevertheless, issues and obstacles have been identified by applying the approach in industry. They are related to tool-specific issues hindering the reliable collection of test execution data as basis for the proposed optimisation approach, the need to exclude of test cases and source code with side-effects from the evaluation with mutation analysis, high run-time requirements for performing the optimizations, as well as discrepancies in coverage measurements between different coverage tools that may even result in an unintended coverage loss in the optimization process.

To get a better understanding of the potential negative effects of these issues in test suite reduction in a practice, we plan to apply the proposed genetic algorithm also on test suites from other projects using different tools and technologies. This work has already been started, leading to the observation of further obstacles resulting from custom test runners interfering with the execution of optimized test suites. Thus, we see the need to devote further work to investigate test suite reduction in industry environments.

Acknowledgements. This work was partially supported by the Austrian Research Promotion Agency (FFG) in the frame of the COMET competence center SCCH [892418].

82   P. Stadler et al.

References

1. Yoo, S., Harman, M.: Regression testing minimization, selection and prioritization: a survey. Softw. Test. Verif. Reliab. **22**(2), 67–120 (2012)
2. Engström, E., Runeson, P.: A qualitative survey of regression testing practices. In: Ali Babar, M., Vierimaa, M., Oivo, M. (eds.) PROFES 2010. LNCS, vol. 6156, pp. 3–16. Springer, Heidelberg (2010). https://doi.org/10.1007/978-3-642-13792-1_3
3. Gmeiner, J., Ramler, R., Haslinger, J.: Automated testing in the continuous delivery pipeline: a case study of an online company. In: 2015 IEEE Eighth International Conference on Software Testing, Verification and Validation Workshops (ICSTW), pp. 1–6. IEEE (2015)
4. Elbaum, S., Rothermel, G., Penix, J.: Techniques for improving regression testing in continuous integration development environments. In: Proceedings of the 22nd ACM SIGSOFT International Symposium on Foundations of Software Engineering, pp. 235–245 (2014)
5. Shi, A., Zhao, P., Marinov, D.: Understanding and improving regression test selection in continuous integration. In: IEEE 30th International Symposium on Software Reliability Engineering (ISSRE), vol. 2019, pp. 228–238. IEEE (2019)
6. Khan, S.U.R., Lee, S.P., Javaid, N., Abdul, W.: A systematic review on test suite reduction: approaches, experiment's quality evaluation, and guidelines. IEEE Access **6**, 11816–11841 (2018)
7. Engström, E., Runeson, P., Skoglund, M.: A systematic review on regression test selection techniques. Inf. Softw. Technol. **52**(1), 14–30 (2010)
8. Khatibsyarbini, M., Isa, M.A., Jawawi, D.N., Tumeng, R.: Test case prioritization approaches in regression testing: a systematic literature review. Inf. Softw. Technol. **93**, 74–93 (2018)
9. He, Z.F., Sheng, B.K., Ye, C.Q, et al.: A genetic algorithm for test-suite reduction. In: 2005 IEEE International Conference on Systems, Man and Cybernetics, vol. 1, pp. 133–139. IEEE (2005)
10. Ma, X., Sheng, B., Ye, C.: Test-suite reduction using genetic algorithm. In: Cao, J., Nejdl, W., Xu, M. (eds.) APPT 2005. LNCS, vol. 3756, pp. 253–262. Springer, Heidelberg (2005). https://doi.org/10.1007/11573937_28
11. Nachiyappan, S., Vimaladevi, A., SelvaLakshmi, C.: An evolutionary algorithm for regression test suite reduction. In: 2010 International Conference on Communication and Computational Intelligence (INCOCCI), pp. 503–508. IEEE (2010)
12. Wang, S., Ali, S., Gotlieb, A.: Minimizing test suites in software product lines using weight-based genetic algorithms. In: Proceedings of the 15th Annual Conference on Genetic and Evolutionary Computation, pp. 1493–1500 (2013)
13. Wieringa, R.J.: Design Science Methodology for Information Systems and Software Engineering. Springer, Heidelberg (2014). https://doi.org/10.1007/978-3-662-43839-8
14. Buchgeher, G., Ernstbrunner, C., Ramler, R., Lusser, M.: Towards tool-support for test case selection in manual regression testing. In: 2013 IEEE Sixth International Conference on Software Testing, Verification and Validation Workshops, pp. 74–79. IEEE (2013)
15. Ramler, R., Salomon, C., Buchgeher, G., Lusser, M.: Tool support for change-based regression testing: an industry experience report. In: Winkler, D., Biffl, S., Bergsmann, J. (eds.) SWQD 2017. LNBIP, vol. 269, pp. 133–152. Springer, Cham (2017). https://doi.org/10.1007/978-3-319-49421-0_10
16. Goldberg, D.E.: Genetic Algorithms. Pearson Education, London (2013)

17. Kramer, O.: Genetic Algorithms. In: Genetic Algorithm Essentials, pp. 11–19. Springer, Cham (2017). https://doi.org/10.1007/978-3-319-52156-5
18. Orso, A., Shi, N., Harrold, M.J.: Scaling regression testing to large software systems. ACM SIGSOFT Softw. Eng. Notes **29**(6), 241–251 (2004)
19. Haider, A.A., Nadeem, A., Akram, S.: Safe regression test suite optimization: a review. In: 2016 International Conference on Open Source Systems & Technologies (ICOSST), pp. 7–12. IEEE (2016)
20. Ali, N., et al.: On the search for industry-relevant regression testing research. Empir. Softw. Eng. **24**(4), 2020–2055 (2019). https://doi.org/10.1007/s10664-018-9670-1
21. Duan, K., Fong, S., Siu, S.W., Song, W., Guan, S.S.U.: Adaptive incremental genetic algorithm for task scheduling in cloud environments. Symmetry **10**(5), 168 (2018)
22. Alemerien, K., Magel, K.: Examining the effectiveness of testing coverage tools: an empirical study. Int. J. Softw. Eng. Appl. **8**(5), 139–162 (2014)
23. Horváth, F., Gergely, T., Beszédes, Á., Tengeri, D., Balogh, G., Gyimóthy, T.: Code coverage differences of java bytecode and source code instrumentation tools. Softw. Qual. J. **27**, 79–123 (2019)

Software Metrics

A Catalog of Source Code
Metrics – A Tertiary Study

Umar Iftikhar$^{(\boxtimes)}$, Nauman Bin Ali, Jürgen Börstler, and Muhammad Usman

Blekinge Institute of Technology, Karlskrona, Sweden
umar.iftikhar@bth.se
https://www.bth.se

Abstract. *Context:* A large number of source code metrics are reported in the literature. It is necessary to systematically collect, describe and classify source code metrics to support research and practice.

Objective: We aim to utilize existing secondary studies to develop a catalog of source code metrics together with their descriptions. The catalog will also provide information about which units of code (e.g., operators, operands, lines of code, variables, parameters, code blocks, or functions) are used to measure the internal quality attributes and the scope on which they are collected.

Method: We conducted a tertiary study to identify secondary studies reporting source code metrics. We have classified the source code metrics according to the measured internal quality attributes, the units of code used in the measures, and the scope at which the source code metrics are collected.

Results: From 711 secondary studies, we identified 52 relevant secondary studies. We reported 423 source code metrics together with their descriptions and the internal quality attributes they measure. Source code metrics predominantly incorporate *function* as a unit of code to measure internal quality attributes. In contrast, several source code metrics use more than one unit of code when measuring internal quality attributes. Nearly 51% of the source code metrics are collected at the *class* scope, while almost 12% and 15% of source code metrics are collected at *module* and *application* levels, respectively.

Conclusions: Researchers and practitioners can use the extensive catalog to assess which source code metrics meet their individual needs based on the description and classification scheme presented.

Keywords: Internal quality attributes · Code measurement · Code quality · Tertiary study · Source code metrics

1 Introduction

During software development or evaluating open-source components before incorporating them into the codebase, measuring the quality of the software product is essential. One of the objective methods to measure the quality of a software product is through source code metrics.

© The Author(s), under exclusive license to Springer Nature Switzerland AG 2023
D. Mendez et al. (Eds.): SWQD 2023, LNBIP 472, pp. 87–106, 2023.
https://doi.org/10.1007/978-3-031-31488-9_5

Fenton and Bieman [19] classify quality attributes of a software product into internal and external quality attributes. Internal quality attributes of the source code relate to source code characteristics without accounting for the execution environment. In contrast, external quality attributes relate to how the source code behaves in the context of a specific environment. Several studies have shown a link between internal quality attributes and underlying issues in source code, such as code smells [27] and code decay [8]. Similarly, studies have also measured internal quality attributes to investigate the impact of code refactoring [29]. By assessing the internal attributes of the codebase regularly, practitioners can avoid introducing anti-patterns and incurring technical debt.

Source code metrics are often used to measure the internal quality attributes of the software. Several source code metrics have been proposed over the years. Some of the popular metric suites include Halstead metrics [20], McCabe complexity metric [37], Chidamber & Kemerer (CK) metrics [15] and Li & Henry metrics [34]. Source code metrics are utilized in several cases, e.g., defect proneness [23], bug prediction [42], assessing domain-specific software [49], and in evaluating the implementation of software product lines [36].

Source code metrics use information regarding a software product's structure and size and provide numerical values mapped to quality attributes [33]. While measuring, source code metrics target various units of code. These units of code are measured at different scope levels (e.g., at application, class, module, or function level) to gain insight into specific aspects and areas of code. As an illustrated example, *number of methods (NOM)* is described as "count of all the methods defined in a class" [9]. In this case, we measure the size of the source code by measuring a unit of code *method*, and the scope of the measurement is at the *class* level.

The large number of secondary studies reporting source code metrics provides an opportunity to collect and categorize source code metrics. Through a tertiary study, we aim to provide an extensive catalog of source code metrics reported in secondary studies, their descriptions, and classifications. The catalog of source code metrics, along with definitions and measured internal attributes, the scope of measurement can be a starting point in identifying and selecting suitable source code metrics for the specific measurement needs of researchers and practitioners.

In our previous work [25], we investigated the strength of the evidence linking source code metrics with internal and external quality attributes from 15 secondary studies. The aim of the current tertiary study is to provide an extensive catalog of the source code metrics reported in secondary studies.

The paper is structured as follows. Section 2 presents the related work, followed by Sect. 3 on methodology. We discuss the threats to validity in Sect. 4 and the results in Sect. 5. Section 6 summarizes our reflections on the results while Sect. 7 concludes the review.

2   Related Work

Several systematic studies have synthesized source code metrics reported in the literature. Nunez et al. [39] conducted a mapping study that classified more than 300 source code metrics according to four programming paradigms, supported extraction tools, systems used for benchmarking and topics studied from primary studies between 2010 and 2015. However, the study does not report descriptions of the source code metrics.

Saraiva et al. [43] identified 67 aspect-oriented source code metrics to measure software maintainability and reported 15 aspect-oriented metrics reported by at least two primary studies. The study is limited to only one quality attribute, i.e., maintainability, and does not report aspect-oriented metrics for other quality attributes. Hernandez-Gonzalez et al. [21] focused only on design-level metrics and summarized 26 design-level source code metrics from 15 primary studies. Caulo et al. [13] proposed a taxonomy of 512 metrics that can be used for software fault prediction. These studies have specified limited scope and thus do not provide a holistic classification of the source code metrics along with their descriptions.

Arisholm et al. [6] proposed a classification of dynamic coupling metrics based on granularity, entity, and scope, though their study is limited to dynamic coupling metrics only.

In contrast, several studies provide descriptions of the frequently used source code metrics, including Briand et al. [11], Sharma et al. [45], Kaur et al. [28] but only include descriptions for the source code metrics which are part of a source code metric suite.

Lacerda et al. [31] have conducted a tertiary study on a closely related topic of code smells and refactoring. While the tertiary study does not report any source code metrics, the secondary studies included several source code metrics for code smell detection and comparing refactoring improvements. As mentioned in Sect. 3.1, we have included the secondary studies reported by Lacerda et al. [31] in the list of publications considered for selection criteria.

To our knowledge, no systematic study reports a catalog of source code metrics and classifies them by units of code and scope. We report source code metrics aggregated in secondary studies, with no limitations on the years a secondary study was published and without limiting the scope to a particular programming paradigm. We also report descriptions of all the source code metrics extracted in these studies. A comparison of the secondary and tertiary studies on the subject is provided in Table 1.

3   Methodology

We used the guidelines by Kitchenham et al. [30] in this tertiary study to answer the following research question:

Table 1. Comparison of secondary and tertiary studies on source code metrics

Studies	Source	Years covered	Focus	Limitations
Saraiva et al. [44]	138 primary studies	1992–2011	Aspect-oriented metrics for maintainability	Other quality attributes, e.g., reliability are not in the scope
Nunez et al. [39]	226 primary studies	2010–2015	Source code metrics for AOP, OOP, FOP, tools used, datasets used	Component-based metrics are not reported, source code metrics definitions are not provided
Hernandez-Gonzalez et al. [21]	15 primary studies	1997–2016	Design level metrics	Scope focused on design level metrics; search years covered, primary studies used are not reported
Caulo et al. [13]	196 primary studies	1991–2017	Metrics for fault prediction	Scope focused on fault-prediction source code metrics only
Our earlier study [25]	15 secondary studies	1985–2020 (based on the included primary studies)	Strength of evidence linking source code metrics and quality attributes	Only investigate reported link between source code metrics and external quality attributes
Present study	52 secondary studies on source code	1976–2020 (based on the included primary studies)	Catalog of source code metrics to measure quality attributes, report various uses of source code metrics, e.g., bad smells detection	Secondary studies used as the source

RQ 1: *Which source code metrics are used in the secondary studies to measure internal (code quality) attributes?*

RQ 1.1: *Which units of code are used to measure the internal (code quality) attributes?*

RQ 1.2: *At which scope are the internal (code quality) attributes measured?*

3.1 Search Strategy

We followed the guidelines by Petersen et al. [41] and searched in one indexing (Scopus) and two publisher databases (IEEE Xplore and ACM digital library). ACM and IEEE are among the most relevant publishers of research in software engineering [14,48] while Scopus is one of the largest indexing services covering published articles from several publishers [3,10]. Source code metrics are often reported in the context of measuring quality attributes. Thus, we utilized a keyword-based search [4,30] as our primary search strategy. The search string consisted of six blocks; the first block contains synonyms for source code, the second block focuses on quality attributes measured, and the third block restricts the search results to systematic studies. The remaining three blocks limit the search results to articles and conference papers in the area of computer science written in English. We also incorporated synonyms for metrics, such as "measure" and "indicator" to improve the search string.

As depicted in Fig. 1, we identified keywords from ISO/IEC 25010:2011 [38] and a set of 14 relevant papers already known to the authors due to their domain expertise (see *KnownSetOfPapers* in the online supplement [24]) to formulate our search string given in Table 2. The search string in Table 2 was also adapted to ACM and IEEE.

We used a set of 11 secondary studies (see *Validation set(QGS)* in the online supplement [24]) as a quasi-gold standard (QGS) [30] to evaluate the effectiveness of the search string. Two authors independently formulated the QGS, which included of 11 secondary studies [47]. We executed the search string in February 2021, which captured eight of the 11 (precision 1.46% and recall 73%) studies mentioned in the QGS. To improve the search coverage, we supplemented our search results with the secondary studies covered by Lacerda et al. [31] as they are relevant to our topic (these studies are italicized in Table 8). After removing duplicates, we found 711 unique publications (see Fig. 2).

Table 2. Search string used for automated search in the study

Search string
TITLE-ABS-KEY ((("code" OR "software program" OR "software product" OR "software application" OR "software system" OR "object oriented" OR "aspect oriented" OR "feature oriented")
AND
("quality" OR "smell*" OR "pattern" OR "functional suitability" OR "performance" OR "efficiency" OR "compatibility" OR "usability" OR "reliability" OR "security" OR "maintainability" OR "portability" OR "analyzability" OR "modifiability" OR "testability" OR "compliance" OR "stability" OR "comprehension" OR "understandability" OR "understanding" OR "maintenance" OR "modularity" OR "reusability" OR "changeability" OR "evolvability" OR "modification" OR "testability" OR "evolution" OR "readability" OR "metric*" OR "measur*" OR "indicator" OR "refactoring"))
AND
("systematic review" OR "systematic literature review" OR "systematic map" OR "systematic mapping" OR "tertiary study" OR "tertiary review" OR "mapping study" OR "multivocal literature review" OR "multivocal literature mapping"))
AND
(LIMIT-TO (DOCTYPE , "re") OR LIMIT-TO (DOCTYPE , "ar") OR LIMIT-TO (DOCTYPE , "cp"))
AND
(LIMIT-TO (SUBJAREA , "COMP") OR LIMIT-TO (SUBJAREA , "ENGI"))
AND
(LIMIT-TO (LANGUAGE , "English"))

3.2   Selection Process

We used the criteria described in Table 3 to select relevant papers from the search results. Papers fulfilling the Boolean expression (C0 AND C1 AND C2 AND (C3 OR C4)) were selected for full-text reading. We retained papers for the next phase if there were indications that the full text of a paper might contain relevant information. Papers that only fulfilled C5 were excluded.

As a first step, the first author excluded publications with less than eight pages and not written in English. We excluded systematic studies with less than eight pages as such studies are unlikely to report sufficiently detailed literature review methods and results. Out of the 711 search results in Fig. 2, the first

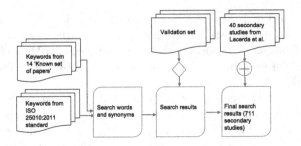

Fig. 1. Search string generation and validation steps

author identified 163 publications that did not meet the page and language requirements according to Table 3 and were excluded.

Table 3. Inclusion/exclusion criteria used in the tertiary study

	Inclusion Criteria
C0	Publications in English language and with length of at least eight pages
C1	Peer-reviewed workshop, journal or conference publications
C2	Publications claiming to have systematically studied available literature, i.e., systematic literature studies (SLRs or SMSs) or multivocal literature studies (MLRs, MLMs)
C3	Papers that identify, describe source code metrics to measure internal quality attributes or determine levels of code quality (e.g., work on quality measurement or code smells)
C4	Papers that relate source code metrics/quality attributes/code refactoring/code smells to external quality attributes
	Exclusion Criteria
C5	Publications that are about only external quality attributes of software product/system/service, or about the quality of other artifacts like defect reports, test code, or test cases i.e., studies not related to source code metrics

We conducted a pilot round of the selection process [2,30] to improve its objectivity and to develop a shared understanding of the topic. The piloting step involved all four authors and 12 randomly selected papers from the search results, which were assessed independently by all authors as *relevant*, *irrelevant*, or *maybe relevant*. An initial agreement percentage of 58% was achieved, which is moderate. To reduce the chances of misalignment between authors and to improve the moderate initial agreement, the selection criteria were discussed during a meeting to improve the shared understanding.

From the remaining 548 secondary studies, the first author applied the selection criteria to all secondary studies, while the second, third, and fourth author were randomly assigned 182 secondary studies each, thus ensuring that each publication is reviewed by two authors. Decision making process suggested by [2,26], was utilised. A secondary study was excluded if it was resolved as "irrelevant" and it was included if it was agreed upon as "maybe" or "included" by both authors. The initial agreement among the author-pairs was 73%. The average

Cohen-Kappa inter-rater agreement between author-pairs was 0.64, which is substantial agreement [17,32]. The disagreements during this round were resolved through discussion. After the study selection based on title and abstract, 413 secondary studies were excluded.

We have used a modified adaptive reading method [40] to conclude the relevance of papers included in the previous step. We read the paper's research questions, introduction, and conclusion sections to decide its relevance. The selection criteria listed in Table 3 were used to ascertain the relevance. The second author reviewed all papers excluded in this stage to reduce the likelihood of excluding a relevant publication. During the adaptive reading of the secondary studies, 36 secondary studies were further identified as not meeting the selection criteria. These excluded studies were reviewed by the second author leading to 99 secondary studies being retained for full-text reading.

During the full-text reading stage, the full text for one secondary study [46] was not available (besides our best efforts), thus, it was excluded. Two papers were identified as the same secondary studies [50,51], and the most recent of the two secondary studies [50] was retained. The first author further identified 40 secondary studies as irrelevant to the scope, which the second and fourth authors reviewed. The authors agreed on excluding 38 secondary studies. After discussion, the remaining two secondary studies were included giving 59 secondary studies for quality assessment and data extraction.

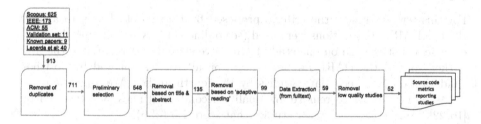

Fig. 2. Selection process results (The count depicts included secondary studies at each stage)

3.3   Data Extraction

Table 4 presents the data extraction form used.

Piloting of the Data Extraction. To validate the data extraction form, the first and third authors independently extracted the data from a randomly selected secondary study from the validation set [24]. The authors agreed on 76% of the data extracted for one randomly selected paper. The differences were discussed and resolved. The threats related to data validity are further discussed in Sect. 4.

Table 4. Data extraction form used in the study

Data Extracted
– Metadata: (author, title, publication venues, publication date)
– Search: (time period covered in the search)
– Source code quality attribute that are the secondary study's focus: (from the research questions)
– Name and acronym of the source code metric (any metrics for which the measured entity is source code or its attributes).
– Description of the source code metric[a]
– Name of the external quality attribute/sub-attribute (i.e., maintainability, reliability, security, functionality, performance, compatibility, usability, or portability [19,38]) measured by the source code metric
– Name of the internal quality attribute (i.e., coupling, cohesion, complexity, inheritance, or size [19]) measured by the source code metric.
– Programming paradigm
– Application domain

[a] when no description of the source code metric was available in the secondary study, we searched in the referenced primary studies.

Validation of the Data Extraction. After data extraction by the first author on all included secondary studies, the fourth author randomly reviewed 5% source code metrics, internal quality attributes, and classifications assigned. The fourth author agreed with 55% of the data entries, while there were "minor issues" with 25% and 20% data entries highlighted as "major issues." The authors discussed the issues in a meeting, and the first author took remedial action to resolve the highlighted minor and major issues throughout the dataset.

3.4   Quality Assessment of the Secondary Studies

For this tertiary study, the criteria proposed by Budgen et al. [12] to answer the five DARE [1] questions were used (see online [24]). After piloting the quality assessment criteria on one study to improve shared understanding, the first author applied the DARE quality criteria on all studies followed by post-hoc validation on 10% secondary studies by the fourth author. We used the quality assessment score to remove low-quality secondary studies [30]. Inspired by [16,22], we removed secondary studies that score 1.5 (of 5).

After removing secondary studies with scores less than or equal to 1.5, 52 secondary studies remained. As DARE is not designed to evaluate the quality of multi-vocal reviews, quality assessment-based selection was not applied to MLRs. The secondary studies removed due to low DARE scores are listed online [24]. Detailed results of quality assessment are also reported online [24].

3.5   Categorization of Source Code Metrics

We read all the source code metric names and their descriptions to identify the units of code measured and the scope at which the values of source code metrics are reported. We used a bottom-up approach to identify the units of code stated in the source code metric descriptions. The definitions of the units of code are shown in Table 5 while the definition of scope are available online [24]. To identify unique source code metrics, we referred to the descriptions of the source code metric. Source code metrics with the same descriptions are treated as duplicates and are combined.

Table 5. Descriptions of units of code used for categorization

Name	Description
Operators	This includes mathematical, assignment and logical operation
Operands	This includes inputs and variables needed to perform a mathematical, logical or assignment operation
Variables	For our classification, they include attributes or variable declarations
Lines of code	A single source code statement. This include composite code statements, logical lines of code, executable lines of code, commands, point cut declarations
Comments	Comments that are part of the source code files
Parameters	Parameters include the parameters declared in method declaration, definition and its implementation
Code Blocks	Code block which span more than a line of code. It could be several lines of code inside a function, code expressions, conditional blocks of code, switch statements and variation point that span several lines of code
Functions	The methods (public, private, protected, abstract, virtual, setters, getters) or operations in a class, procedures or routines (procedural programming languages), advices (aspect oriented programming), refined/constant/base features (feature oriented programming (FOP))
Function Calls	This includes the different method calls, message requests between classes, modules, packages or components
Classes	We include sub-classes, super classes, classes that use instances of other classes, inherited classes, parent classes, children classes, cross-cutting concerns (aspect oriented programming (AOP)), base/constant/refined features classes (feature oriented programming (FOP))
Modules	We use this terminology to loosely classify collection of classes, components, packages, libraries, sub-packages, sub-systems
Others	In the case where the software construct being measured is not clearly stated, or when stated construct is a feature or concern

4 Threats to Validity

In the discussion below, we use the classification of threats by Ampatzoglou et al. [5].

Study Selection. During study selection, we included steps to improve the objectivity of the process. We carefully designed the inclusion/exclusion criteria before the selection process. All authors participated in the pilot rounds, and at least two authors evaluated the relevance of each secondary study. The inter-rater agreement was calculated and reported for all author pairs. All secondary studies that were excluded in the adaptive reading and full-text reading phases by the first author were reviewed by the second author. Since we excluded secondary studies with less than eight pages, some source code metrics may be excluded from our catalog. However, we believe the number of excluded source code metrics to be small and unlikely to change the overall results significantly.

Data Validity. The third author validated the data extraction form designed after discussion. We also piloted the data extraction as recommended by Kitchenham et al. [30] on 10% of the secondary studies. A post-hoc data validation was performed on randomly selected 5% secondary studies with corrective actions taken to resolve the differences. As the data extraction from secondary studies is a manual process, there is a possibility of errors in data extraction given the large data extracted for the given study.

Research Validity. We have reported the search string used, databases used, and the inclusion/exclusion criteria to improve the repeatability of the tertiary study. We regularly updated the design document of the tertiary study and recorded all intermediate results in the protocol document.

Double Counting. Double counting of extracted data can occur in a tertiary study when included secondary studies use the same primary study as their source of information. It may lead to overstating a particular result when a tertiary study aggregates findings from multiple secondary studies that utilized the same primary studies. To avoid double counting, we preferred not to perform any quantitative aggregations of results across secondary studies.

5   Results and Analysis

Of the 52 included secondary studies reporting source code metrics (see Table 8), 31 are systematic literature reviews (SLRs), 20 are systematic mapping studies (SMSs), and one is a multi-vocal literature review (MLM). The earliest study was published in 2009, and 69% (36 out of 52) were published 2015–2020.

The included secondary studies report 423 source code metrics which measure internal quality attributes at different scopes. Due to space limitations, the complete list is available online [24]. Figure 3 shows a screenshot of the online catalog. CK metrics are among the most commonly reported source code metrics. Apart from the CK metrics suite, other frequently reported metric suites include McCabe, and QMOOD metrics.

Among the included secondary studies, 59% (31 out of 52) secondary studies report source code metrics for specific programming paradigms such as aspect-oriented (AOP), feature-oriented (FOP), procedural, and object-oriented (OOP). Source code metrics used in OOP are reported in 46% (24 out of 52) of the secondary studies, while source code metrics used in AOP are reported in 12% (six out of 52) of the secondary studies. Eight (15%) secondary studies report source code metrics used in the procedural paradigm, while source code metrics used in FOP are reported in three secondary studies. Over 50 source code metrics are reported for more than one programming paradigm.

The secondary studies use source code metrics to assess external quality attributes (27 secondary studies), evaluate software-product line implementations (four secondary studies), measure the impact of code refactoring (two secondary studies), and detect source code smells (five secondary studies).

5.1   Internal Quality Attributes

The secondary studies report 14 quality attributes measured by source code metrics which we mapped into six internal quality attributes, as shown in Table 6. The descriptions of the internal quality attributes [24] are based on Fenton and Bieman [19] and Bansiya and Davis [9]. Coupling, size, and complexity are the

Metric ID	Metric Name	Metric Description	Acronym	Code Unit	Scope	Cohesion	Complexity	Coupling	Inheritance	Size	Others
M91	Scattering Of Variation Points	This Metric Measures How Many Variation Points Are Affected By A Feature Constant	SDvp	Code Block	Class	-	-	-	-	-	Y
M92	Concern Diffusion Over Lines Of Code	This Metric Measures The Number Of Transition Points (Transition Points Are Points In The Code Where There Is A "Concern Switch".) For Each Concern Through The Lines Of Code(Sharkawy2019)	CDLOC	Code Block	Others	-					Y
M93	Scattering Of Variation Point Groups	Count The Occurrences Of Similar Variation Point Groups,	SDvpg	Code Block	Code Blc	-					Y
M94	Attribute Hiding Factor	Ahf Is Defined As The Ratio Of The Sum Of The Invisibilities Of All Attributes Defined In All Classes To The Total Number Of Attributes Defined In The System Under Consideration.(Sharma And Dubey 2012)	AHF	Variables	Class	-					Y
M95	Classified Class Data Accessibility	Description: This Metric Measures The Direct Accessibility Of Classified Class Attributes Of A Particular Class And Aims To Protect The Classified Internal Representations Of A Class, I.E., Class Attributes, From Direct Access. (Vogel2021)	CCDA	Variables	Class	-					Y
M96	Classified Instance Data Accessibility	Description: This Metric Measures The Direct Accessibility Of Classified Instance Attributes Of A Particular Class And Helps To Protect The Classified Internal Representations Of A Class, I.E., Instance Attributes, From Direct Access.(Vogel2021)	CIDA	Variables	Class	-					Y
M97	Data Access Metric	This Metrics Is The Ratio Of The Number Of Private (Protected) Attributes To The Total Number Of Attributes Declared In The Class. A High Value Of Dam Is Desired. (Range 0 To 1) (Bansiya And Davis 2002)	DAM	Variables	Class	-					Y
M98	Measure Of Aggregation	This Metric Measures The Extent Of The Part-Whole Relationship, Realised By Using Attributes. The Metric Is A Count Of The Number Of Data Declarations Whose Types Are User Defined Classes. (Bansiya And Davis 2002)	MOA	Variables	Class	-					Y
M99	Conceptual Similarity Between A Method And Class	The Average Of The Conceptual Similarities Between Method Mk And All The Methods From Class Cj.(Poshyvank 2006) (Kagdi 2013)	CSEMC, CS	Functions	Class	-		Y			
M100	Class Inheritance Factor	Class Inheritance Factor Is The Fraction Of The Total Number Of Extended Classes To The Total Number Of Available Classes Defined In A Version Of OO Software. (Vinobha 2014)	CIF	Classes	Class	-			Y		
M101	Critical Superclasses Inheritance	Description: The Metric Is Defined As The Ratio Of The Sum Of Classes That Can Inherit From Each Critical Superclass To The Number Of Possible Inheritances From All Critical Classes In A Class Hierarchy.(Vogel2021). Class Specialization Index: (Nooc * Dit) / Total Methods.(Dick And Sadia 2006)	CSI	Classes	Class	-			Y		
M102	Critical Superclasses Proportion	Description: This Metric Is The Ratio Of The Number Of Critical Superclasses To The Total Number Of Critical Classes In An Inheritance Hierarchy.(Vogel 2021)	CSP	Classes	Class	-			Y		
M103	Association-On Degree	Association On Degree Measures The Association Of Component On The Rest Of The System. (Sartipi 2001)	AoD	Modules	Module	-		Y			

Fig. 3. Screenshot of the online catalog of source code metrics

most frequently reported internal quality attributes, with 161 source code metrics reporting coupling and 78 source code metrics reporting the complexity of the source code. Complexity is the most frequently reported internal quality attribute, with 88% (46 out of 52) secondary studies reporting source code metrics for it. Certain source code metrics are commonly reported. Frequently reported inheritance metrics include *Depth of inheritance tree (DIT)* and *Number of Children (NOC)*. Similarly, frequently reported complexity metrics include *Weighted method per class (WMC)*, *McCabe's cyclomatic complexity (CC)*, and *Response for a class (RFC)*.

5.2 Units of Code in Source Code Metrics to Measure Internal Quality Attributes

We identified 26 units of code utilized in the source code metrics descriptions, which we mapped to 13 categories of units of code [24]. Source code metrics either use a single unit of code or a combination of two or more units of code to measure the reported internal quality attribute. Out of the 423 source code metrics that measure an internal quality attribute, 25% (107 out of 423) of the source code metrics incorporate multiple units of code to measure internal quality attributes. Standalone units of code are more frequently used than composite units of code, with 75% of source code metrics using standalone units of code. *functions* (106 source code metrics) and *classes* (69 source code metrics) are among the most

Table 6. Number of unique source code metrics (column *Metrics*) reported in included secondary studies, categorized by commonly referred internal quality attributes (column *Attribute*)

Attribute	Metrics	Studies
Cohesion	56	S01, S02, S03, S05, S06, S07, S08, S09, S10, S11, S13, S14, S15, S16, S17, S18, S19, S20, S22, S24, S25, S26, S27, S28, S29, S30, S31, S32, S34, S36, S37, S38, S41, S42, S44, S46, S47, S49, S50, S51
Complexity	78	S01, S02, S03, S05, S06, S07, S08, S09, S10, S11, S12, S13, S14, S15, S16, S17, S18, S19, S20, S21, S22, S23, S24, S25, S26, S27, S28, S29, S30, S31, S32, S33, S34, S36, S37, S38, S40, S41, S42, S43, S46, S47, S48, S49, S50, S51
Coupling	161	S01, S02, S03, S05, S06, S07, S08, S09, S10, S11, S13, S14, S15, S16, S17, S18, S19, S20, S22, S23, S24, S25, S26, S27, S28, S29, S30, S31, S32, S34, S36, S37, S38, S40, S41, S43, S44, S45, S46, S47, S49, S50, S51
Inheritance	34	S01, S02, S03, S05, S06, S07, S08, S09, S10, S11, S13, S14, S15, S16, S17, S19, S20, S22, S24, S25, S26, S27, S28, S29, S30, S31, S34, S36, S37, S38, S41, S44, S46, S47, S48, S49, S50, S51
Size	61	S01, S02, S03, S05, S06, S08, S09, S10, S11, S12, S13, S15, S16, S17, S19, S20, S21, S22, S23, S24, S25, S26, S27, S28, S29, S30, S31, S32, S33, S34, S35, S36, S37, S38, S40, S41, S42, S43, S44, S46, S47, S48, S49, S51, S52
Others	33	S01, S02, S05, S06, S08, S09, S11, S16, S17, S19, S20, S24, S25, S26, S27, S29, S31, S34, S36, S37, S38, S45, S49, S51

frequently used standalone units of code. Among the frequently used composite units of code, *classes & functions* (25 source code metrics), and *functions & variables* (34 source code metrics) are used together. The frequently used units of code vary for different internal quality attributes. Source code metrics for coupling predominantly use *classes*, and *functions & variables*. In contrast, size-related source code metrics rely equally on *lines of code*, *classes*, in addition to *functions*. Complexity-focused source code metrics analyze the *code blocks*, *operators & operands*, and *functions* to measure source code's complexity.

5.3   Scope of Source Code Metric Evaluation

The identified scope [24] categorize the source code at six levels of abstraction: *application - module - class - function - code-block - lines of code*. The results of the scope are depicted in Table 7. Source code metrics are most frequently evaluated at the *class* level, followed by *module* and *application* levels. Among source code metrics that report internal quality attributes, 216 evaluate source code metrics at the *class* level. Evaluation of source code metrics at the *class* level is the predominant trend when the scope of individual internal quality attributes is analyzed, followed by evaluation at the *others* and *application* level. Coupling metrics have the highest percentage, 102 out of 161 (63%), among reported internal quality attributes to be evaluated at the *class* level. Intuitively, none of the source code metrics are evaluated at *lines of code*. Only a small subset of source code metrics (three source code metrics) are assessed below the *function* level, suggesting that the lowest meaningful scope is at the *function* level.

One method to utilize the catalog is filtering the source code metrics list using the internal quality attribute of interest, required scope, and unit of code.

The results can act as a good starting point for determining source code metrics available for the specific needs of the catalog user. As an example, selecting complexity as the internal quality attribute of choice, scope as function, and unit of code as code blocks provides 21 source code metrics and their descriptions.

Table 7. Scope identified for source code metrics in secondary studies

Scope	Cohesion	Complexity	Coupling	Inheritance	Size	Others	Total
Application	6	16	16	6	15	3	62
Module	10	8	22	2	4	3	49
Class	30	23	102	20	26	15	216
Functions	4	11	1	1	4	0	21
Code Blocks	0	1	0	0	1	1	3
Others	6	19	20	5	11	11	72
Total	56	78	161	34	61	33	423

6 Discussion

Our tertiary review provides a catalog of source code metrics and their descriptions for researchers and practitioners. We classified the source code metrics based on units of code used to measure internal quality attributes and the scope at which the measured values are reported. We have reported six internal quality attributes measured by source code metrics in the included studies. However, we did not find any source code metrics for internal quality attributes such as messaging and hierarchies, as defined in [9]. It suggests that the two internal quality attributes are less relevant to the included secondary studies' scope, and the two internal quality attributes have received less focus in the literature. Our results show that almost 38% of the reported source code metrics relate to coupling and nearly 18% measure complexity. Arvanitoue et al. [7] also observe complexity and coupling as the most studied internal quality attributes.

Our results show that the CK metrics suite [15] is one of the most frequently used metric suites, which is consistent with other studies (e.g. [39]). Compared to Nunez et al.'s SMS [39], we report more unique source code metrics (423 in comparison to 300) and provide descriptions for source code metrics that may aid researchers and practitioners alike.

One of the challenges in source code metrics is the lack of standardization of names and descriptions. Several studies [18,35,44] have highlighted the inconsistency of metrics' names and acronyms, which may lead to a proliferation of source code metrics. We report 61 unique source code metrics referred to in the literature with more than one acronym (e.g., *cyclomatic complexity* is assigned several acronyms such as *CC, cyclo, MVG,* and *V(G)*). In the cases where the metric's name is not specified along with the acronym, it may mislead the audience. Using metrics' names and descriptions, we further identified 150 source code metrics that use similar units of code while aggregating the units of code at different scope levels (e.g., lines of code, lines of feature code, lines of concern code). We considered these as essentially similar source code metrics and reported them as similar source code metrics accordingly. However, we observed that the lack of standardization of names of source code metrics remains an open issue. This affects the utility provided by various source code metrics.

We observe that the units of code and scope vary when a particular programming paradigm is considered. Intuitively, such a variation is expected as different programming paradigms focus more on certain scopes than others. We note that source code metrics for feature-oriented programming are predominantly measured at the feature level or concern level, which we have classified as *others*. The most often measured units of code for procedural languages are *operators & operands*, which are more frequently assessed at the *application* level. Source code metrics reported for the object-oriented programming paradigm measure *functions* as units of code and predominantly collect metrics at the *class* level of scope. One possible reason for the difference is that applications written in procedural languages have different code structure compared to object-oriented applications, and the size of the application being investigated may also vary.

In the included studies, we observed a lack of source code metrics explicitly designed for contemporary programming languages, such as Python, Go, and Kotlin. While several open-source measurement tools exist, summarising these source code metrics may improve the utilization of appropriate source code metrics for contemporary programming languages.

Please note that the catalog currently does not provide information about which reported measurement tools also support source code metrics. Future work can report the available tool support for the reported source code metrics to improve the usability of the catalog for practitioners.

7   Conclusions

We analyzed 52 systematic studies reporting 423 unique source code metrics, which we have compiled into a catalog. We have intentionally excluded metrics related to change, architecture, and testing for the catalog. We have categorized the source code metrics in the catalog according to the units of code and the scope.

Our results show that source code metrics predominantly measure function-level units of code such as methods, advices, procedures, and routines. Furthermore, source code metrics frequently report values at the *class* level instead of higher scope levels, such as at the *module* or *application* level.

When reporting the catalog of source code metrics, we have not considered the validation status of the presented source code metrics. One of the future works can supplement the catalog to include the validation status of the reported source code metrics, thus improving the usability of the catalog.

Acknowledgment. This work has been supported by ELLIIT, a Strategic Area within IT and Mobile Communications, funded by the Swedish Government. The work has also been supported by the OSIR project funded by the Swedish Knowledge Foundation (grant number 20190081).

Appendix

Table 8. List of included secondary studies (PS: No. of primary studies, QS: Quality score)

#	Title	Study type	Publ year	PS	Start year	End year	QS	Focus
S01	A Systematic Literature Review on Bad Smells-5 W's: Which, When, What, Who, Where	SLR	2021	351	1990	2017	2.5	Bad Smells
S02	Evolution of quality assessment in SPL: A systematic mapping	SMS	2020	63	2000	2019	2.5	Design Approach Evaluation
S03	A systematic literature review on empirical studies towards prediction of software maintainability	SLR	2020	36	1990	2019	4	Maintainability
S04	Evaluating code readability and legibility: An examination of human-centric studies	SLR	2020	54	2016	2019	3	Maintainability
S05	Software smell detection techniques: A systematic literature review	SLR	2020	145	1993	2018	3	Bad Smells
S06	A Tool-Based perspective on software code maintainability metrics: A Systematic Literature Review	SLR	2020	43	2000	2019	3	
S07	A systematic review of software usability studies	SLR	2020	150	1990	2016	4	Usability
S08	Metrics in automotive software development: A systematic literature review	SLR	2020	38	1990	2018	3	Source code metrics
S09	Machine learning techniques for software bug prediction: A systematic review	SLR	2020	31	2014	2020	2.5	Reliability
S10	How does object-oriented code refactoring influence software quality? Research landscape and challenges	SMS	2019	142	2000	2017	4.5	Refactoring
S11	Metrics for analyzing variability and its implementation in software product lines: A systematic literature review	SLR	2019	29	2007	2017	3.5	Source code metrics
S12	Software quality assessment model: a systematic mapping study	SMS	2019	31	1998	2015	3	Quality assessment models and measurement
S13	A survey on software testability	SMS	2019	208	1982	2017	2	Maintainability
S14	A survey on software coupling relations and tools	SLR	2019	136	2002	2017	2.5	Internal quality attributes
S15	Software quality measurement in software engineering project: A systematic literature review	SLR	2019	38	1984	2005	2	Quality assessment models and measurement
S16	A systematic literature review and meta-analysis on cross project defect prediction	SLR	2019	30	2008	2015	4	Reliability

(continued)

Table 8. (*continued*)

#	Title	Study type	Publ year	PS	Start year	End year	QS	Focus
S17	Empirical studies on software product maintainability prediction: A systematic mapping and review	SMS	2019	82	2000	2018	4	Maintainability
S18	A systematic literature review on the detection of smells and their evolution in object-oriented and service-oriented systems	SLR	2019	78	2000	2017	4	Bad Smells
S19	A Systematic Literature Review on empirical analysis of the relationship between code smells and software quality attributes	SLR	2019	74	1997	2018	5	Bad Smells
S20	Software change prediction: A systematic review and future guidelines	SLR	2019	38	2000	2019	4.5	Maintainability
S21	The impact of code smells on software bugs: A systematic literature review	SLR	2018	18	2007	2017	2.5	Bad Smells
S22	Mapping the field of software life cycle security metrics	SMS	2018	71	2000	2017	3	Security
S23	Smells in software test code: A survey of knowledge in industry and academia	MLM	2019	166	2001	2016	-	Bad Smells
S24	Coupling and cohesion metrics for object-oriented software: A systematic mapping study	SMS	2018	129	1991	2017	2	Internal quality attributes
S25	Empirical evaluation of the impact of object-oriented code refactoring on quality attributes: A systematic literature review	SLR	2018	76	2001	2015	4.5	Refactoring
S26	A systematic review on search-based refactoring	SLR	2017	71	2000	2016	2.5	Refactoring
S27	Software maintainability: Systematic literature review and current trends	SLR	2016	96	1991	2015	3.5	Maintainability
S28	Metrics and statistical techniques used to evaluate internal quality of object-oriented software: A systematic mapping	SMS	2016	79	2004	2013	2	Internal quality attributes
S29	Software change prediction: A literature review	SLR	2016	20	1998	2011	2.5	Maintainability
S30	Open source software evolution: A systematic literature review (part 1 2)	SLR	2016	190	1997	2016	2	Software Evolution
S31	Empirical evidence on the link between object-oriented measures and external quality attributes: A systematic literature review	SLR	2015	99	1996	2011	4.5	Muliple External Attributes
S32	Software metrics for measuring the understandability of architectural structures - A systematic mapping study	SMS	2015	25	1990	2013	4	Maintainability
S33	How have we evaluated software pattern application? A systematic mapping study of research design practices	SMS	2015	27	2000	2014	4.5	Design Patterns
S34	Software fault prediction: A systematic mapping study	SMS	2016	70	2002	2014	2	Reliability
S35	Software product size measurement methods: A systematic mapping study	SMS	2014	208	1982	2014	2	Internal quality attributes
S36	*Empirical evidence of code decay: A systematic mapping study*	*SMS*	*2013*	*30*	*1999*	*2013*	*4*	*Bad Smells*

(*continued*)

Table 8. (*continued*)

#	Title	Study type	Publ year	PS	Start year	End year	QS	Focus
S37	A systematic mapping study on software product line evolution: From legacy system re-engineering to product line refactoring	SMS	2013	74	1997	2012	2.5	Software Evolution
S38	Software fault prediction metrics: A systematic literature review	SLR	2013	106	1990	2011	4	Reliability
S39	Software clone detection: A systematic review	SLR	2013	213	1997	2011	3.5	Bad Smells
S40	A mapping study to investigate component-based software system metrics	SMS	2013	36	2000	2010	3.5	Source code metrics
S41	A systematic review of the empirical validation of object-oriented metrics towards fault-proneness prediction	SLR	2013	29	1995	2012	4	Reliability
S42	A systematic review of quality attributes and measures for software product lines	SLR	2012	35	1996	2012	3	Source code metrics
S43	A systematic review of studies of open source software evolution	SLR	2010	41	1976	2009	2.5	Software Evolution
S44	A systematic review of comparative evidence of aspect-oriented programming	SLR	2010	22	1997	2008	4	Source code metrics
S45	Software architecture degradation in open source software: A systematic literature review	SLR	2020	74	2000	2019	4	Bad Smells
S46	A mapping study on design-time quality attributes and metrics	SMS	2017	154	1976	2015	2.5	Source code metrics
S47	What's up with software metrics? - A preliminary mapping study	SMS	2010	100	2000	2005	2	Source code metrics
S48	A systematic review of software maintainability prediction and metrics	SLR	2009	15	1985	2008	4	Maintainability
S49	Source code metrics: A systematic mapping study	SMS	2017	226	2010	2015	4	Source code metrics
S50	A survey of search-based refactoring for software maintenance	SMS	2018	50	1999	2016	3	Refactoring
S51	A review of code smell mining techniques	SLR	2015	46	1999	2015	3	Bad Smells
S52	*Software design smell detection: a systematic mapping study*	*SMS*	*2018*	*395*	*2000*	*2017*	*3*	*Bad Smells*

References

1. The Centre for Reviews and Dissemination (CRD) Database of Abstracts of Reviews of Effects (DARE). https://www.crd.york.ac.uk/CRDWeb/. Accessed 20 Oct 2022
2. Ali, N.B., Petersen, K.: Evaluating strategies for study selection in systematic literature studies. In: Proceedings of the 8th ACM/IEEE International Symposium on Empirical Software Engineering and Measurement, pp. 1–4 (2014)
3. Ali, N.B., Tanveer, B.: A comparison of citation sources for reference and citation-based search in systematic literature reviews. e-informatica Soft. Eng. J. **16**, 220106 (2022)
4. Ali, N.B., Usman, M.: Reliability of search in systematic reviews: towards a quality assessment framework for the automated-search strategy. Inf. Softw. Technol. **99**, 133–147 (2018)

5. Ampatzoglou, A., Bibi, S., Avgeriou, P., Chatzigeorgiou, A.: Guidelines for managing threats to validity of secondary studies in software engineering. In: Contemporary Empirical Methods in Software Engineering, pp. 415–441. Springer, Cham (2020). https://doi.org/10.1007/978-3-030-32489-6_15
6. Arisholm, E., Briand, L., Foyen, A.: Dynamic coupling measurement for object-oriented software. IEEE Trans. Softw. Eng. **30**(8), 491–506 (2004)
7. Arvanitou, E., Ampatzoglou, A., Chatzigeorgiou, A., Galster, M., Avgeriou, P.: A mapping study on design-time quality attributes and metrics. J. Syst. Softw. **127**, 52–77 (2017)
8. Bandi, A., Williams, B., Allen, E.: Empirical evidence of code decay: a systematic mapping study. In: Proceedings - Working Conference on Reverse Engineering, WCRE, pp. 341–350 (2013)
9. Bansiya, J., Davis, C.G.: A hierarchical model for object-oriented design quality assessment. IEEE Trans. Softw. Eng. **28**(1), 4–17 (2002)
10. Barros-Justo, J.L., Benitti, F.B., Matalonga, S.: Trends in software reuse research: a tertiary study. Comput. Stand. Interfaces **66**, 103352 (2019)
11. Briand, L.C., Wüst, J.: Empirical studies of quality models in object-oriented systems. Adv. Comput. **56**, 97–166 (2002)
12. Budgen, D., Brereton, P., Williams, N., Drummond, S.: What support do systematic reviews provide for evidence-informed teaching about software engineering practice?. e-informatica Softw. Eng. J. **14**(1), 7–60 (2020)
13. Caulo, M., Scanniello, G.: A taxonomy of metrics for software fault prediction. In: 2020 46th Euromicro Conference on Software Engineering and Advanced Applications (SEAA), pp. 429–436. IEEE (2020)
14. Chen, L., Babar, M.A., Zhang, H.: Towards an evidence-based understanding of electronic data sources. In: 14th International Conference on Evaluation and Assessment in Software Engineering (EASE), pp. 1–4 (2010)
15. Chidamber, S.R., Kemerer, C.F.: A metrics suite for object oriented design. IEEE Trans. Softw. Eng. **20**(6), 476–493 (1994)
16. Curcio, K., Santana, R., Reinehr, S., Malucelli, A.: Usability in agile software development: a tertiary study. Comput. Stand. Interfaces **64**, 61–77 (2019)
17. El Emam, K.: Benchmarking kappa: interrater agreement in software process assessments. Empir. Softw. Eng. **4**(2), 113–133 (1999)
18. El-Sharkawy, S., Yamagishi-Eichler, N., Schmid, K.: Metrics for analyzing variability and its implementation in software product lines: a systematic literature review. Inf. Softw. Technol. **106**, 1–30 (2019)
19. Fenton, N., Bieman, J.: Software Metrics: A Rigorous and Practical Approach. CRC Press, Boca Raton (2019)
20. Halstead, M.H.: Elements of Software Science. Elsevier Science Ltd., Amsterdam (1977)
21. Hernandez-Gonzalez, E.Y., Sanchez-Garcia, A.J., Cortes-Verdin, M.K., Perez-Arriaga, J.C.: Quality metrics in software design: a systematic review. In: Proceedings of the 7th International Conference in Software Engineering Research and Innovation, pp. 80–86 (2019)
22. Hoda, R., Salleh, N., Grundy, J., Tee, H.M.: Systematic literature reviews in agile software development: a tertiary study. Inf. Softw. Technol. **85**, 60–70 (2017)
23. Hosseini, S., Turhan, B., Gunarathna, D.: A systematic literature review and meta-analysis on cross project defect prediction. IEEE Trans. Softw. Eng. **45**(2), 111–147 (2019)

24. Iftikhar, U., Ali, N.B., Börstler, J., Usman, M.: Dataset for a catalog of source code metrics - a tertiary study. https://doi.org/10.5281/zenodo.7219870. Accessed 20 Oct 2022

25. Iftikhar, U., Ali, N.B., Börstler, J., Usman, M.: A tertiary study on links between source code metrics and external quality attributes. Information and Software Technology (Submitted)

26. Jabangwe, R., Börstler, J., Šmite, D., Wohlin, C.: Empirical evidence on the link between object-oriented measures and external quality attributes: a systematic literature review. Empir. Softw. Eng. **20**(3), 640–693 (2015)

27. Kaur, A.: A systematic literature review on empirical analysis of the relationship between code smells and software quality attributes. Arch. Comput. Methods Eng. **27**(4), 1267–1296 (2019). https://doi.org/10.1007/s11831-019-09348-6

28. Kaur, A., Kaur, K., Pathak, K.: A proposed new model for maintainability index of open source software. In: Infocom Technologies and Optimization Proceedings of 3rd International Conference on Reliability, pp. 1–6 (2014)

29. Kaur, S., Singh, P.: How does object-oriented code refactoring influence software quality? Research landscape and challenges. J. Syst. Softw. **157**, 110394 (2019)

30. Kitchenham, B.A., Budgen, D., Brereton, P.: Evidence-Based Software Engineering and Systematic Reviews, vol. 4. CRC Press, Boca Raton (2015)

31. Lacerda, G., Petrillo, F., Pimenta, M., Guéhéneuc, Y.G.: Code smells and refactoring: a tertiary systematic review of challenges and observations. J. Syst. Softw. **167**, 110610 (2020)

32. Landis, J.R., Koch, G.G.: The measurement of observer agreement for categorical data. Biometrics 33, 159–174 (1977)

33. Lanza, M., Marinescu, R.: Object-Oriented Metrics in Practice: Using Software Metrics to Characterize, Evaluate, and Improve the Design of Object-Oriented Systems. Springer, Cham (2007)

34. Li, W.: Another metric suite for object-oriented programming. J. Syst. Softw. **44**(2), 155–162 (1998)

35. Malhotra, R., Chug, A.: Software maintainability: systematic literature review and current trends. Int. J. Softw. Eng. Knowl. Eng. **26**(08), 1221–1253 (2016)

36. Martins, L., Afonso, P.J., Freire, A., Costa, H.: Evolution of quality assessment in SPL: a systematic mapping. IET Softw. **14**(6), 572–581 (2020)

37. McCabe, T.J.: A complexity measure. IEEE Trans. Softw. Eng. **2**(4), 308–320 (1976)

38. de Normalización, O.I.: ISO-IEC 25010: 2011 systems and software engineering-systems and software quality requirements and evaluation (square)-system and software quality models. International Organization for Standardization, Geneva, Switzerland (2011)

39. Nuñez-Varela, A.S., Pérez-Gonzalez, H.G., Martínez-Perez, F.E., Soubervielle-Montalvo, C.: Source code metrics: a systematic mapping study. J. Syst. Softw. **128**, 164–197 (2017)

40. Petersen, K., Feldt, R., Mujtaba, S., Mattsson, M.: Systematic mapping studies in software engineering. In: 12th International Conference on Evaluation and Assessment in Software Engineering (EASE) 12, pp. 1–10 (2008)

41. Petersen, K., Vakkalanka, S., Kuzniarz, L.: Guidelines for conducting systematic mapping studies in software engineering: an update. Inf. Softw. Technol. **64**, 1–18 (2015)

42. Saharudin, S., Wei, K., Na, K.: Machine learning techniques for software bug prediction: a systematic review. J. Comput. Sci. **16**(11), 1558–1569 (2020)

43. Saraiva, J., et al.: Aspect-oriented software maintenance metrics: a systematic mapping study. IET Semin. Digest **2012**(1), 253–262 (2012)

44. Saraiva, J., Soares, S., Castor, F.: Towards a catalog of object-oriented software maintainability metrics. In: 2013 4th International Workshop on Emerging Trends in Software Metrics (WETSoM), pp. 84–87. IEEE, San Francisco, CA (2013)

45. Sharma, A., Dubey, S.K.: Comparison of software quality metrics for object-oriented system. Int. J. Comput. Sci. Manage. Stud. (IJCSMS) **12**, 12–24 (2012)

46. Sreeji, K., Lakshmi, C.: A systematic literature review: recent trends and open issues in software refactoring. Int. J. Appl. Eng. Res. **10**(18), 39696–39707 (2015)

47. Tran, H.K.V., Börstler, J., bin Ali, N., Unterkalmsteiner, M.: How good are my search strings? Reflections on using an existing review as a quasi-gold standard. e-Informatica Softw. Eng. J. **16**(1), 220103 (2022)

48. Turner, M.: Digital libraries and search engines for software engineering research: an overview. Keele University, UK (2010)

49. Vogel, M., et al.: Metrics in automotive software development: a systematic literature review. J. Softw. Evol. Process **33**(2), e2296 (2021)

50. Yan, M., Xia, X., Zhang, X., Xu, L., Yang, D., Li, S.: Software quality assessment model: a systematic mapping study. Sci. China Inf. Sci. **62**(9), 1–18 (2019). https://doi.org/10.1007/s11432-018-9608-3

51. Yan, M., Xia, X., Zhang, X., Xu, L., Yang, D.: A systematic mapping study of quality assessment models for software products. In: 2017 International Conference on Software Analysis, Testing and Evolution (SATE), pp. 63–71. IEEE (2017)

Software Quality Assurance

Software Quality Assessment: Defect Life Cycle, Software Defect Profile, Its Types and Misalignments

Oleksandr Gordieiev[1,2]([⊠]) [iD], Daria Gordieieva[1,2] [iD], and Austen Rainer[1] [iD]

[1] Queen's University Belfast, Belfast BT9 5BN, UK
{o.gordieiev,d.gordieieva,a.rainer}@qub.ac.uk
[2] Lutsk National Technical University, Lutsk 43018, Ukraine

Abstract. In order to understand the causes and consequences of software defects, it is necessary to investigate a software defect life cycle. This article proposes a general structure of the software defect life cycle model. A more detailed analysis of the life cycle of a defect makes it possible to present its modifications in the form of pathological chains. During the injection of software defects, not only are individual software defects used, but also their various sets in the form of a software defect profile. The software defect profile consists of a taxonomy of types of defects and factual defects distributed according to these types. During defect injection, certain changes in the software defect profile occur in the form of inconsistencies in terms of the types of defects and their quantity. Such inconsistencies are called misalignments. Based on the analysis of misalignments in the software defect profile, conclusions about the software quality and the software assessment process quality are drawn. Throughout its life cycle, the software defect profile undergoes several changes from injection to an analysis of test results. As a result of such changes, different types of profiles are formed. The analysis of the mismatches of the types of software defect profiles made it possible to determine the full set of possible variants of such misalignments. In general, the article presents results at a more theoretical level with some small examples.

Keywords: software defect injection · software defect profile · software defect life cycle · software defect profile misalignments

1 Introduction and Formulation of the Problem

Software development is inextricably linked to and depends on the software quality assurance process. The primary task of software quality assurance is the assessment of quality. Since the starting point of the development of software engineering [1], many different approaches, methods, techniques and tools have been developed for software quality assessment. The approach to quality assessment, which is based on the injection of software defects, has been used for decades. This approach is based on the artificial injection of defects into the software and its further testing. Defect injection is used to assess the quality of testing (processes, groups of testers, test suites), fault tolerance mechanisms and finding hidden defects. Recently, the importance of using such an approach has increased due to the inclusion of defect injection techniques in known international standards [2] as mandatory for application in the development of critical software. Despite the simplicity of understanding the software quality assessment approach based on defect injection, there are many unsolved or partially solved tasks for its implementation in the form of separate models, methods and tools. Such tasks include the description and the presentation of the defect life cycle model and the software defect profile [3] and the influence of the analysis of the misalignments of the obtained software defect profiles on decision-making regarding the level of software quality in general, etc. A *software defect* is a result that has certain causes and consequences. The causes, as a rule, are mistakes of developers, and the consequences can be expressed in faults or failures of information systems. A *software defect profile* is an ordered set of defects consisting of a software defect profile taxonomy and specific defects that correspond to it. A *misalignment of software defect profile* is the inconsistency between types of defect profiles in part of specific software defects, for example, between a profile of injected software defects and a profile of software discovered defects.

Software defects have been analyzed and studied since the emergence of software engineering as a separate engineering direction [1]. Since that time, the direction of software quality assurance has crystallized and it is successfully developing within software engineering. Many approaches, methods, techniques and tools were developed to ensure software quality. Despite this, problems with the appearance of software defects still exist today [4, 5]. According to the authors of the article, when the studying software defects, it is advisable, primarily, to research the software defect itself in more detail and describe its life cycle as part of the software development process. Known models describing the software defect life cycle have a number of disadvantages. For example, the defect flow chart and defect life cycle [6, 7] are more general and mostly illustrative (graphic). The existing works do not fully consider the software defect in detail [8, 9], do not research it at all or do not fully consider the cause-and-effect relationships of the appearance of software defects [10, 11]. The software defect life cycle (SDFLC) in context with the software development life cycle [12, 13] was not reviewed as well.

Articles devoted to software quality assessment using software defect injection are quite diverse in their goals and tasks. In article [14], in part of a model of the feasibility of using defect injection for software quality assessment, only the problem of assessing the expediency of defect injecting is raised, but there is no presentation in the form of a separate model or method. Misalignments in the profile of software defects in existing works are usually considered as a comparison of the profile of defects that are injected and the profile of defects detected during software testing [15]. Software defect profile life cycle and software defect profile misalignments did not receive a detailed and formal description [16], however, the need for a deeper study of the types of profiles of software defects and software defect profile life cycle is considered in the articles [14–16].

In this regard, the **goal of the article** is a detailed presentation and description of the life cycle of a software defect, as well as to study different variants of the misalignments of software defect profiles during software defect injection for software quality assessment.

The article is logically divided into two parts: the first (Sect. 2) is the presentation and the description of the software defect life cycle as a white box, and the second

(Sects. 3–4) is the presentation and the description of the software defect profile, its types and misalignments as well as the analysis of its misalignments in the software quality assessment process using defect injection. I.e. the concept of the material presentation is as follows: at the beginning the software defect life cycle, its pathological chains and defect life cycle in a V-shaped model were represented. The following is a software defect profile, its types and variants of misalignments. The article ends with a simple example and conclusions.

2 Software Defect Life Cycle

The software defect life cycle will be considered based on the following basic sequence «developer mistake - software failure»: developer's (operator's) *mistake* (white background), software *defect* or *bug* (light gray background), calculation *error* (light gray background) during software operation, *fault* and *failure* (black background) (see Fig. 1).

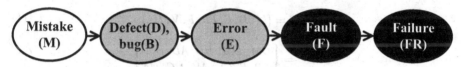

Fig. 1. Sequence «developer's mistake - software failure»

Based on the sequence «developer's mistake – software failure», we will form the basic structure of a software defect life cycle. Such structure includes the following basic components: sources (causes) (white background), results (light gray background), aftermaths (black background) and side effects (dark gray background) (see Fig. 2). For better identification of the elements of the figures, the background scheme of designations for Fig. 2 will be similar for subsequent figures - developments of the software defect life cycle. First of all, for the result to occur – a defect (D) and a calculation error (E) - there must be a cause or source, as a rule, these are mistakes (M) of developers or operators. A defect in the software leads to a calculation error. The aftermaths of a calculation error are a fault (F) or a failure (FR). It is also worth noting that software defects can lead to a vulnerability (V), through which attackers can gain unauthorized access (UA) to the software and ultimately lead to fault or failure (see Fig. 2). Thus, the set of elements of SDFLC consists of 7 elements and will have the following view (1).

A more detailed analysis of SDFLC made it possible to detail it and form the so-called modifications of SDFLC, which were called «pathological chains». Pathological chains are a sequence of interconnected events that can occur during the development and use of human-computer systems software, starting from a developer's (operator's) mistake and ending with the failure of the information system as a whole. Let us consider the structure of the pathological chain. It includes the following elements: operator's (or developer's) mistake (OM), development mistake (DM), hidden defect in software (HD), active defect in software (AD), error calculation (E), fault (F), failure (FR), created vulnerability (CV), activated vulnerability (AV), unauthorized control (UC), unauthorized access to data (UA) (Fig. 3).

Thus, the set of elements of the pathological chain, the modification of the life cycle of a software defect, has expanded to 11 elements and will already have the following refined form (2).

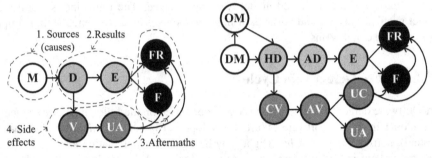

Fig. 2. General structure of SDFLC   **Fig. 3.** Structure of the pathological chain

$$SDFLC = \{M, D, E, FR, F, V, UA\} \qquad (1)$$

$$SDFLC = \left\{ \begin{array}{l} OM, DM, HD, AD, E, \\ FR, F, CV, AV, UC, UA \end{array} \right\} \qquad (2)$$

There are physical, design, coding and interaction pathological chains. Let us consider them in more detail:

1. Physical pathological chain. The nature of the origin of this chain is physical, that is, it is physical defects or malfunctions of the hardware. The elements of such a chain will be denoted by an index - the letter «p» (physical) (Fig. 4). The set of elements of such a chain is practically identical to the set of elements of a unified structure. A new element is added to the physical pathological chain – hardware wear (HW) (white background). It is believed that hardware wear is also a source of software defects (Fig. 4). Note that the set of elements of the pathological chain, the modification of the SDFLC, has increased to 12 elements and has had the following refined form (3). An example of a defect corresponding to this pathological chain and models of impact hardware defect to software are described in [17].

2. Design pathological chain. For this pathological chain, design defects will be considered. The elements of such a chain will be denoted by an index – the letters «des» (design) (see Fig. 5). The set of elements of the design pathological chain, the modification of the software defect life cycle, will have the following specified form (4). An example impact mistake in software design corresponding to the design pathological chain and its impact on software defect is described in [18].

$$SDFLC_p = \left\{ \begin{array}{l} OM_p, DM_p, HD_p, AD_p, E_p, FR_p, \\ F_p, HW_p, CV_p, AV_p, UC_p, UA_p \end{array} \right\} \qquad (3)$$

$$SDFLC_{des} = \left\{ \begin{array}{l} OM_{des}, DM_{des}, HD_{des}, AD_{des}, E_{des}, \\ FR_{des}, F_{des}, CV_{des}, AV_{des}, UC_{des}, UA_{des} \end{array} \right\} \qquad (4)$$

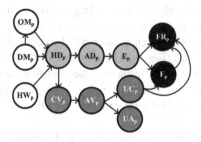

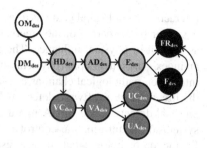

Fig. 4. Physical pathological chain   **Fig. 5.** Design pathological chain

3. Coding pathological chain. Software coding defects will be considered here. The elements of such a chain will be denoted by an index - the letters «cod» (coding) (see Fig. 6). The set of elements of the coding pathological chain, the modification of the software defect life cycle, will have the following form (5). Examples of software coding defect types corresponding to this pathological chain is described in [19].

4. Interaction pathological chain. In this pathological chain, it is the interaction defects in the information system that are implied. The elements of such a chain will be denoted by an index - the letter «i» (interaction) (Fig. 7). The set of elements of the interaction pathological chain, modification of the software defect life cycle, will have the following form (6). This is a general pathological chain, which is detailed by several pathological chains associated with hardware wear or complete (partial) failure of hardware, as well as with informational influence as a result of cyber attacks.

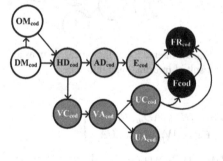

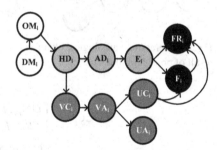

Fig. 6. Coding pathological chain   **Fig. 7.** Interaction pathological chain

$$SDFLC_{cod} = \left\{ \begin{array}{l} OM_{cod}, DM_{cod}, HD_{cod}, AD_{cod}, E_{cod}, \\ FR_{cod}, F_{cod}, CV_{cod}, AV_{cod}, UC_{cod}, UA_{cod} \end{array} \right\} \qquad (5)$$

$$SDFLC_i = \left\{ \begin{array}{l} OM_i, DM_i, HD_i, AD_i, E_i, \\ FR_i, F_i, CV_i, AV_i, UC_i, UA_i \end{array} \right\} \qquad (6)$$

Several types can be distinguished in the general interaction pathological chain. These include:

a. Interaction pathological chain as a result of physical influence. In general the chain is similar to the nature of the emergence of an interaction pathological chain, but as a result of physical influence. The elements of such a chain will be denoted by an index - the letters «pi» (physical interaction) (Fig. 8). The set of elements of the interaction pathological chain as a result of physical influence, the modification of the life cycle of a software defect, will have the following form (7). For example, physical defects of the FPGA module can affect the interaction with information systems or the information-control system.

b. Interaction pathological chain as a result of informational influence. The nature of the origin of this chain, in general, is similar to the nature of the emergence of an interaction pathological chain, but with clarification - as a result of informational influence. The elements of such a chain will be denoted by an index - the letter «ii» (information interaction) (see Fig. 9). The set of elements of the interaction pathological chain as a result of the informational influence, the modification of the life cycle of a software defect, will have the following form (8). An example of such a pathological chain can be a successful cyber attack on an information system, as a result of which the attacking party gets the opportunity to influence to replace or to distort information.

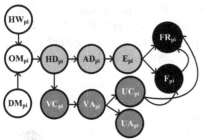

Fig. 8. Interaction pathological chain as a result of physical influence

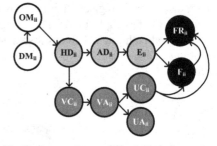

Fig. 9. Interaction pathological chain as a result of informational influence

$$SDFLC_{pi} = \begin{Bmatrix} OM_{pi}, DM_{pi}, HD_{pi}, AD_{pi}, E_{pi}, \\ FR_{pi}, F_{pi}, CV_{pi}, AV_{pi}, UC_{pi}, UA_{pi} \end{Bmatrix} \qquad (7)$$

$$SDFLC_{ii} = \begin{Bmatrix} OM_{ii}, DM_{ii}, HD_{ii}, AD_{ii}, E_{ii}, \\ FR_{ii}, F_{ii}, CV_{ii}, AV_{ii}, UC_{ii}, UA_{ii} \end{Bmatrix} \qquad (8)$$

It is worth noting that the SDFLC is not always linear (one-level), in the form in which it is graphically presented in Fig. 1, 2, 3, 4, 5, 6, 7, 8 and 9. Such non-linearity is associated with the evolution of software defects within the software development life cycle. For example, let us consider the evolution of a defect according to the V-shaped model, which is used in the development of critical software. The defect may appear at the first stage «1. Planning of project and requirements» and be a software requirement defect (gradient background). When verifying the requirements at stage «2. Analysis of product requirements» such a defect may not be detected, that is, it will become a hidden defect (dotted background). Evolving, the defect can move to the next stage of development «3. Software architecture development» (cross background) or to «4. Detailed design» (background with vertical lines) or even further - to the stage «5. Coding» (background with oblique lines). Such evolution of a software defect can be carried out from stage to stage of the software development life cycle, until it manifests itself during the execution or testing of the developed software (see Fig. 10). Thus, the defect can evolve from HD_1 to HD_5 (marked with different backgrounds) as they are physically different defects. At stage «5. Coding» the evolution of the software defect also stops at the following stages «6. Modular testing», «7. Integration and testing», «8. System acceptance testing» and «9. Production, operation, support» (all defects are marked with a background with oblique lines). The defect moves from stage to stage of testing inside software until the moment of detection of a software defect. It should be noted that at each stage of software development, a defect from a hidden state (HD) can move to an active state (AD), i.e. it can be detected by testers and fixed.

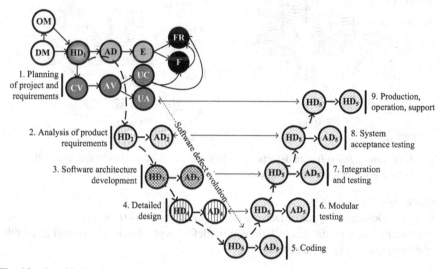

Fig. 10. Graphical representation of software defect evolution taking into account the V-shaped model of software development

3 Software Defect Profile

A software defect profile consists of a software defect profile taxonomy and specific defects that correspond to this taxonomy. That is, each type of defect corresponds to a certain number of real defects. The nomenclature of software defects types and the quantity of software defects are not a constant value and depend on the specific software defect profile. The structure of the taxonomy of software defects types is presented in the hierarchical form (see Fig. 11) or faceted structure (see Fig. 12). Each profile can be described as follows:

– Taxonomy of Profile of Defects ($TPD_{tts(i)}$) - is described by the set of SoftWare Defects Types (taxons) ($SWDT_{tts(i)}$), the Set of Classification FeaTures of software defects ($SCFT_{tts(i)}$), the adjacency table for describing subordination in a hierarchical structure, a correspondence table for establishing correspondence between taxons and classification features in hierarchical and facet structures. Note that tts - a type of taxonomic structure – can take the values H – hierarchical structure or F – faceted structure, i – defect profile number. An example of a software defect profile description as a hierarchical structure is represented (Fig. 11) - $SWDT_{H(i)}$: 1- Coding defects, 1.1 – mathematical defects, 1.1.1 – addition operation, 1.1.2 – subtraction operation, 1.1.3 – division operation, 1.2 – logical defects, 1.2.1 –operation «and», 1.2.2 –operation «or».

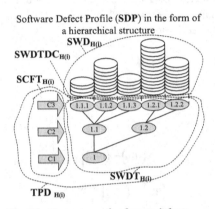

Fig. 11. Taxonomy of software defects types in the form of a hierarchical structure

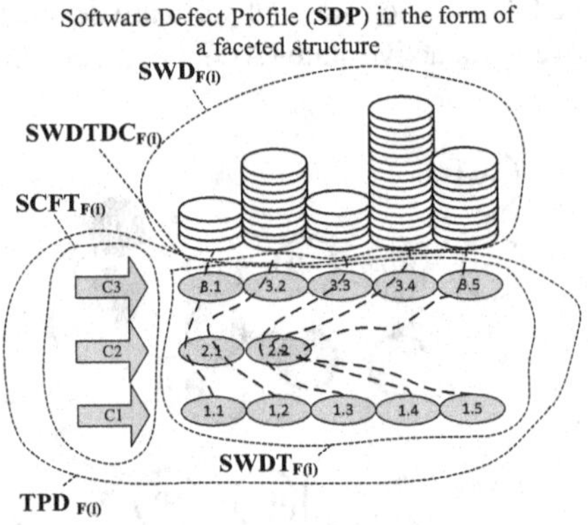

Fig. 12. Taxonomy of software defects types in the form of a faceted structure

– SoftWare Defects ($SWD_{tts(i)}$);
– Software Defects to Types of Defects Correspondence ($SWDTDC_{tts(i)}$), i.e. by the set of corresponding predicates (relationship) «defect-type of defect», as well as a table of descriptions of specific defects.

Thus, the Software Defect Profile (*SDP*) is described by three elements - the taxonomy of the defect profile, the set of defects and the relationship «defect-type of defect» (9).

In turn, the elements of the software defect profile represent the following separate sets – the profile defects taxonomy includes a set of classification features and a set of defects types (10).

$$SDP_i = \{TPD_{tts(i)}, SWD_{tts(i)}, SWDTDC_{tts(i)}\} \tag{9}$$

$$TPD_i = \{SWDT_{tts(i)}, SCFT_{tts(i)}\} \tag{10}$$

Since the classification features are necessary only for the formation of the taxonomy structure, they are not used to describe the actual software defect. It is also worth noting that the actual defects, their types and relations are also separated sets: $SWD = \{swd_i\}_{i=0}^{n}$,

$SWDT = \{swdt_i\}_{i=0}^n$, $SWDTDC = \{swdtdc_i\}_{i=0}^n$. Therefore, each defect is described by the ratio (swdtdc) of the defect (swd) and its type (swdt) as follows (11):

$$swd_i \; swdtdc \; swdt_j, \tag{11}$$

where i – is the actual defect number, j – is the defect type number.

4 Software Defect Profile Types and Software Defects Profile Misalignments

The software defect profile from the moment of its formation to the detection of defects during testing and verification undergoes certain natural changes. Let us consider and describe the life cycle of the software defect profile. To describe the life cycle of the software profile, we introduce the following necessary formulations and sets of defect profiles, the names of which will be equivalent to the names of the profile types:

- Forecasted Taxonomy of Profile of Defects (*FTPD*) – a taxonomy of software defects types that reflects the potential types of defects that may be contained in software. It is usually presented in the form of a hierarchical or faceted structure;
- Forecasted Quantity of Profile of Defects (*FQPD*) – the number of defects that could potentially be in the software;
- Forecasted Profile of Defects (*FPD*) – profile of defects, which represents the correspondence between the predicted taxonomy of software defect types and real defects, the number of which corresponds to the predicted number of software defects. $FPD = \{fpd_i\}_{i=0}^n$ – set of defects of Forecasted Profile of Defects;
- Injected Profile of Defects (*IPD*) is a defects profile that is a subset of the predicted software defect profile. Real defects included in this profile are injected into the software. $IPD = \{ipd_i\}_{i=0}^n$ – set of defects of Injected Profile of Defects;
- Profile of All Discovered Defects (*PADD*) – profile of defects that were discovered during software testing. $PADD = \{padd_i\}_{i=0}^n$ – set of defects of Profile of All Discovered Defects;
- Profile of New Discovered Defects (*PNDD*) – profile of defects that were discovered during testing and are not injected defects. $PNDD = \{pndd_i\}_{i=0}^n$ – set of defects of Profile of New Discovered Defects;
- Profile of Discovered and Injected Defects (*PDID*) – profile of defects that were detected during testing and are previously injected defects. $PDID = \{pdid_i\}_{i=0}^n$ – set of defects of Profile of Discovered and Injected Defects;
- Profile of Not Discovered and Injected Defects (*PNDID*) – profile of defects that were previously injected and not detected during testing. $PNDID = \{pndid_i\}_{i=0}^n$ – set of defects of Profile of Not Discovered and Injected Defects.

We will present and describe different variants of combinations of defects in the resulting software defect profiles before and after testing and verification. Such variants of combinations of defects are the misalignments of types of software defect profiles.

We will assume that the set of defects is a combination of factual (real) defects, each of which corresponds to the type of defects and physically exists. Next, we will present and describe such misalignments in more detail. Table 1 presents the possible variants of profiles misalignments.

Table 1. Variants of misalignments types of software defect profiles

1	2	3	4	5
$IPD \neq FPD$ $IPD \cap FPD \neq \varnothing$ $\lVert FPD \rvert > \lvert IPD \rvert$	$IPD = PADD = PDID$ $PNDD = PNDID = \varnothing$	$IPD \in PADD$ $PNDD = PADD \setminus IPD$ $PDID = IPD$ $PNDID = \varnothing$	$IPD \neq PADD$ $IPD \cap PADD \neq \varnothing$ $\lVert IPD \rvert > \lvert PADD \rvert$	$IPD \neq PADD$ $PNDD = PADD \setminus IPD$ $PDID = IPD \cap PADD$ $IPD \cap PADD \neq \varnothing$ $PNDID = IPD \setminus PADD$ $\lVert IPD \rvert = \lvert PADD \rvert$

6	7	8	9	10
$IPD \neq PADD$ $PNDD = PADD \setminus IPD$ $PDID = IPD \cap PADD$ $IPD \cap PADD \neq \varnothing$ $PNDID = IPD \setminus PADD$ $\lVert IPD \rvert < \lvert PADD \rvert$	$IPD \neq PADD$ $PNDD = PADD \setminus IPD$ $PDID = IPD \cap PADD$ $IPD \cap PADD \neq \varnothing$ $PNDID = IPD \setminus PADD$ $\lVert IPD \rvert > \lvert PADD \rvert$	$IPD \neq PADD$ $IPD \cap PADD = \varnothing$ $PNDD = PADD$ $PDID = \varnothing$ $PNDID = IPD$ $\lVert IPD \rvert = \lvert PADD \rvert$	$IPD \neq PADD$ $IPD \cap PADD = \varnothing$ $PNDD = PADD$ $PDID = \varnothing$ $PNDID = IPD$ $\lVert PADD \rvert > \lvert IPD \rvert$	$IPD \neq PADD$ $IPD \cap PADD = \varnothing$ $PNDD = PADD$ $PDID = \varnothing$ $PNDID = IPD$ $\lVert IPD \rvert > \lvert PADD \rvert$

Example. Let us consider an example of injection of software defects. The object of defect injection is a tool for the support of software requirements profile quality assessment, which is used to assess the quality of the requirements profile. In particular, it is used for assessment of the 5th chapter «Assurance of computer security on stage of development» of the draft of the new standard «Requirements to computer security of NPP Instrumentation and Control Systems (NPP I&C)» developed by the Ukrainian state regulatory body was selected [20].

15 defects of various types were injected into the program code. During the testing of the tool, 17 defects were discovered, of which 14 – injected and discovered during testing (PDID), 1 – injected and not discovered during testing (PNDID), and 3 – new defects (PNDD). Such a variant falls under misalignment № 6 (according to the Table 2). The reason for such a variant is the insufficient completeness and accuracy of the test sets for assessment quality of the set of requirements.

5 Conclusions

In the article the software defect evolution was formally presented, starting with the reasons that led to its occurrence and ending with possible consequences. A more detailed representation of the life cycle model of a software defect in the form of a set of pathological chains allows one to take into account the peculiarities of the variety of states of a software defect.

The article presents and describes the software defect profile and its types during the injection of defects, which make it possible to trace the main transformations of the software defect profile, and the emerging mismatches of the types of software defect profiles allowing a more in-depth assessment of software quality.

It is advisable to direct further research to the study of defects of the second type and the phenomenon of mutation of defects and on the development of the model of software defect analysis focused on assessing the quality of software based on the injecting of software defects. In this direction, a separate task is the study of the life cycle of defects during the development and implementation of defect injection procedures, which are used to assess the functional safety of FPGA projects for local information and control systems of NPPs. At the same time, the software defect life cycle can be clarified, and the number of its modifications can increase.

Of course, a separate future work should be devoted to the presentation and detailed description of a practical case.

Acknowledgment. This research is supported by the British Academy.

References

1. Software Engineering. Report on a conference sponsored by the NATO science committee, Garmisch, Germany, October 1968, http://homepages.cs.ncl.ac.uk/brian.randell/NATO/nato1968.PDF. Accessed 07 Aug 2022
2. NUREG/CR-7151-2012. Development of a Fault Injection-Based Dependability Assessment Methodology for Digital I&C Systems. Volume 1–4. U.S. Nuclear Regulatory Commission
3. Watts, H., Daughtrey, T.: The software quality profile. In: Fundamental Concepts for the Software Quality Engineer, pp. 3–17. American Society for Quality (2002)
4. Gopal, K., Jadoo, S., Ramgoolam, J., Devi, V.: Software quality problems in requirement engineering and proposed solutions for an organization in mauritius. Int. J. Comput. Appl. **137**(2), 23–31 (2016). https://doi.org/10.5120/ijca2016908698
5. Gao, J., Zhang, L., Zhao, F., Zhai, Y.: Research on software defect classification. In: IEEE 3rd Information Technology, Networking, Electronic and Automation Control Conference (ITNEC), New York, pp. 748–754. IEEE Press (2019). https://doi.org/10.1109/ITNEC.2019.8729440
6. Defect Flow Chart. https://creately.com/diagram/example/idva2npq2/defect-flow-chart-classic. Accessed 03 Nov 2023
7. Defect Life Cycle. https://creately.com/diagram/example/jjik56un1/defect-life-cycle. Accessed 03 Nov 2023
8. Shaikh, S., Changan, L., Rasheed, M., Rizwan, S.: Wide research on software defect model with overgeneralization problems. In: 2nd International Conference on Computing, Mathematics and Engineering Technologies (iCoMET), New York, pp. 1–6. IEEE Press (2019). https://doi.org/10.1109/ICOMET.2019.8673510
9. Han, W., Jiang, H., Lu, T., Zhang, X., Li, W.: Software defect model based on similarity and association rule. Int. J. Multimed. Ubiquit. Eng. **10**(7), 1–10 (2015)

10. Frattini, F., Pietrantuono, R., Russo, S.: Reproducibility of software bugs. In: Fiondella, L., Puliafito, A. (eds.) Principles of Performance and Reliability Modeling and Evaluation. SSRE, pp. 551–565. Springer, Cham (2016). https://doi.org/10.1007/978-3-319-30599-8_21
11. Singh, P.: Learning from software defect datasets. In: 5th International Conference on Signal Processing, Computing and Control (ISPCC), New York, pp. 58–63. IEEE Press (2019). https://doi.org/10.1109/ISPCC48220.2019.8988366
12. Rahman, A., Nurdatillah, H.: Defect management life cycle process for software quality improvement. In: 3rd International Conference on Artificial Intelligence, Modelling & Simulation (AIMS-2015), New York, pp. 241–244. IEEE Press (2015). https://doi.org/10.1109/AIMS.2015.47
13. Alba, A.B., Zúber, A.H., Fruchier, J.C.: Verdict analysis and defect life cycle management in test automation environments. In: 8th International Conference on Software Process Improvement (CIMPS), New York, pp. 1–6. IEEE Press (2019). https://doi.org/10.1109/CIMPS49236.2019.9082436
14. Feinbube, L., Pirl, L., Polze, A.: Software fault injection: a practical perspective. In: García Márquez, F.P., Papaelias, M. (eds.) Dependability Engineering, (2017). https://www.intechopen.com/chapters/56668. https://doi.org/10.5772/intechopen.70427. Accessed 27 June 2022
15. Gordeyev, A., Kharchenko, V., Andrashov, A.: Case-based software reliability assessment by fault injection unified procedures. In: International Workshop on Software Engineering in East and South Europe (SEESE), pp. 1–8. Association for Computing Machinery, New York (2008). https://doi.org/10.1145/1370868.1370870
16. Natella, R., Cotroneo, D., Madeira, H.: Assessing dependability with software fault injection: a survey. ACM Comput. Surv. **48**(3), 1–55 (2016). https://doi.org/10.1145/2841425
17. Park, J., Kim, H.-J., Shin, J.-H., Baik, J.: An embedded software reliability model with consideration of hardware related software failures. In: IEEE Sixth International Conference on Software Security and Reliability, New York, pp. 207–214. IEEE Press (2012). https://doi.org/10.1109/SERE.2012.10
18. D'Ambros, M., Bacchelli, A., Lanza, M.: On the impact of design flaws on software defects. In: 10th International Conference on Quality Software, New York, pp. 23–31. IEEE Press (2010). https://doi.org/10.1109/QSIC.2010.58
19. Huckle, T., Neckel, T.: Bits and Bugs: A Scientific and Historical Review of Software Failures in Computational Science. Society for Industrial and Applied Mathematics (2019)
20. Gordieiev, O., Gordieieva, D., Tryfonov, A., Dokukin, V., Odarushchenko, E.: Method and tool for support of software requirements profile quality assessment. In: 11th IEEE International Conference on Dependable Systems, Services and Technologies (DESSERT), New York, pp. 72–79. IEEE Press (2020). https://doi.org/10.1109/DESSERT50317.2020.9125020

Comparing Anomaly Detection and Classification Algorithms: A Case Study in Two Domains

Miroslaw Staron[1]([✉])(iD), Helena Odenstedt Hergés[2,3](iD), Linda Block[3](iD), and Martin Sjödin[3]

[1] Chalmers | University of Gothenburg, Gothenburg, Sweden
miroslaw.staron@gu.se
[2] Sahlgrenska University Hospital, Gothenburg, Sweden
[3] Ericsson AB, Gothenburg, Sweden
{helena.odenstedt,linda.block}@vgregion.se, martin.sjodin@ericsson.se

Abstract. Utilizing large data sets in practical scenarios usually requires identifying, annotating and classifying rare events or anomalies. Although several methods exists, there are two classes of algorithms: anomaly detection algorithms and classification algorithms. Both types of algorithms have different characteristics and in this paper, we set out to compare them on two cases. We use data from a neurointensive care unit and from microwave radio transmissions. We apply Isolation Forest and Random Forest algorithms to find events in the data that occur with a frequency of ca. 1%. The results show that classification algorithms (Random Forest) perform better and can achieve up to 100% accuracy, while the anomaly detection algorithms (Isolation Forest) can achieve only 73% at best. Based on the results, we conclude that it is better to invest in annotating data á priori and use classification algorithms, despite the lower costs of using the anomaly detection algorithms.

Keywords: Machine learning · neuro-intensive care · telecommunication

1 Introduction

Detecting anomalies in data is an important application of machine learning. There are several algorithms and methods specifically designed for this purpose, e.g., Isolation Forest [16], Minimum Covariant Analysis [13] or Local Outlier Detection [2]. These algorithms are usually based on statistical properties of the dataset and identify data points which are different from the other ones. Their main advantage is the ability to identify outliers in any dataset without the need to manually annotate the datapoints. However, their major limitation is that the identified anomalies (outliers) are not based on the domain of the

© The Author(s), under exclusive license to Springer Nature Switzerland AG 2023
D. Mendez et al. (Eds.): SWQD 2023, LNBIP 472, pp. 121–136, 2023.
https://doi.org/10.1007/978-3-031-31488-9_7

dataset, meaning that the outliers can be valid data points, just appearing with a low frequency – so called *rare events*.

On the other hand, there are over 1,000 algorithms for supervised machine learning (not even counting all possible deep learning models/architectures) [8]. These algorithms take annotated data as input and use it to identify dependencies in the data. The main advantage of these algorithms is that they can be trained to recognize data points relevant for the domain. However, the main disadvantage is that these algorithms require human annotators and that the frequency of anomalies plays a significant role in the performance of the algorithms – the more frequent these anomalies are, the better the performances of the trained model.

Although there are studies comparing algorithms for anomaly detection, e.g., the study by Omar et al. [20] or Entanbouly et al. [7], these studies focus on single domains and only on the anomaly detection algorithms. Therefore, in this study, we set out to compare anomaly detection algorithms with classification algorithms in two different domains – telecommunication signal analysis and neuro-critical care. These two cases provide us with the unique opportunity to explore these algorithms on datasets that originate from computer-generated signals (telecommunication) or patients (neuro-intensive care). We focus on the research questions that unites the neuro-critical care and telecommunication signal analysis, namely:

Which machine learning data analysis pipeline is best for rare, specific events in large multidimensional data sets from critically ill patients and Microwave signals?

We address this problem by conducting a case study at two organizations – a collaboration between Ericsson AB (a telecommunication equipment manufacturer) and Sahlgrenska University Hospital (development of algorithms for detection of cerebral ischema). The problem manifests itself differently in both domains, and our goal was to study which of the existing ML (machine learning) techniques can be used in both cases, at the same time as to evaluate the methods for anomaly detection vs. methods for classification. The most interesting part of this study is the ability to use two, very different, types of data – a computer generated network communication signal (which should be predictable given the generation parameters) and a set of signals from patients (which differ given the natural variations between the patients and the characteristics of their conditions).

In addition to the evaluation of the algorithms, we discuss the challenges when applying and comparing algorithms on cross-disciplinary projects. Technology transfer is one of the crucial success factors for software engineering research and development [26] and therefore researchers, working on the development of fundamental technologies, must validate their findings in multiple domains in order to ensure that the technology is robust and generally applicable. By working with two different partners, we contribute with insights on how to increase the portability of results between these two, seemingly different, domains.

The remaining of the paper is structured as follows. Section 2 describes the problem which we use to establish a common collaboration platform. Section 3 describes the algorithms used in our study. Section 4 describes the datasets and the experiment set-up. Section 5 shows the results of applying these two types of algorithms on our data. Finally, Sect. 6 describes the conclusion from our study.

2 Rare Events in Large Datasets – Unifying Problem

Detecting rare and specific events in large data sets is a problem where both machine learning methods and domain applications require in-depth studies [12]. The machine learning challenges lie in the ability to balance classes (specific events are significantly less frequent than the baseline data points) and reducing noise (class and attribute noise). The domain challenges lie in the ability to identify these events (consensus on what a baseline/anomaly/specific event is), describe them (characteristics of the specific event) as well as reducing the effect of confounding factors on the data labelling. In our project, the specific events are: anomalies in the radio signal strengths caused by weather disturbances [5] and cerebral ischemia development in critically ill patients [3, 28].

In critically ill patients, especially in a surgical environment, this problem is experienced when diagnosing specific conditions, in our case cerebral ischemia (stroke). Cerebral ischemia can develop over time, but the event, or period of time associated with this event, is much shorter than other events (e.g. anesthesia, surgery-related events) and needs to be identified from noisy data [14,18]. Multiple physiological signals will be recorded in the critical care setting of patients undergoing thrombectomy, i.e. an endovascular intervention to remove a blood clot in order to restore cerebral circulation. The complexity of physiological data, for example irregularities in Heart Rate Variability (HRV) data, is that it is highly dependent on patient related factors and therefore no algorithms are currently available that can be applied out-of-the-box. The existing methods are still not robust enough for reliable use in a clinical environment [25].

In the telecommunication networks of microwave links, this problem is experienced when finding disturbances in signals [22]. These disturbances can relate to environmental events (e.g. rain, snow [24]), equipment malfunction (e.g. broken antenna [9]) or geographical placement (e.g. radio signal reflection over water). In this project, we aim to find methods that will allow the radio network operators to identify the types of signal disturbances and to reduce the need of costly manual equipment troubleshooting and maintenance such as sending out a technical team to high-altitude antennas.

Figure 1 presents the similarities of the pattern between a NIRS (Near-Infrared Spectroscopy) signal during the clamping of the carotid artery and the drop of radio signal strength caused by a disturbance.

Despite the visible similarities, the two domain applications have differences. First, the variability between entities is different. In the telecommunication domain, as signals are generated by radio antennas, the variability can be predicted (e.g., the frequency is configured for each entity/link, and stays the same during the entire signal transmission). In the healthcare domain, the variability is due to the fact that the signal is generated by a device attached to a patient, and the data can vary due to physiological, medical and clinical factors. Each

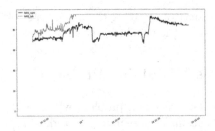

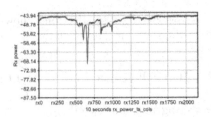

(a) Reduction of the NIRS signal value associated with arterial clamping during carotid surgery. The blue line shows the reduction of oxygen saturation in the right side, no reduction is observed on the left side (orange line)

(b) Reduction of signal strength in a Minilink link between two base stations caused by weather conditions (rain). This is a single signal, which can be complemented by a similar signal from the link going in the opposite direction (to correspond to NIRS left+right).

Fig. 1. Illustration of the similarity of the problem between the patient signal analysis and telecommunication signal analysis.

person has natural variability in the data, e.g., heart rate variability, which is not as stable as the computer-generated telecommunication signal.

Table 1 summarizes the similarities and differences in the two application domains from the perspective of using machine learning. The differences were identified by the research team through observations and discussions with the practitioners.

Table 1. Differences and similarities between the two domains.

Category	ICU	Microwave links
Data collection	automated, through dedicated equipment	automated, through dedicated equipment
Entity	patient	link
Number of signals	5 (NIRS, ABP, EEG, ECG, RESP)	2 (Tx, Rx)
Sampling frequency	250 Hz 500 Hz	0.1 Hz
Number of rare events in a dataset	ca. 8% data points (30 min out of 6 h)	<1% of data points (30 min per week)

The context of two domains, with similarities in data, but differences in the domain, with the access to practitioners from both domains, provides us with a unique opportunity to study the limitations of machine learning methods. In particular, we can study the advantages and disadvantages of anomaly detection algorithms and classification algorithms.

However, in our project, we focus on the comparison between algorithm types, as we want to understand whether it is better to identify rare events by treating them as anomalies or whether these anomalies should be treated as unbalanced classes.

3   Machine Learning Methods Used

Traditionally, machine learning methods used in both domain are similar – they are based on supervised learning and unsupervised learning, e.g., as shown by Komorowski [14] or Musumeci et al. [19]. Therefore, the machine learning pipeline is similar for both domains, as presented in Fig. 2. The pipeline starts with the extraction of data from the measured entities – critically ill patients and microvawe radio links.

Fig. 2. Machine learning pipeline used in our study. The pipeline is used for both algorithms, with the except for labelling, which is not needed for IF.

For the critically ill patients we use a dedicated equipment – Moberg CNS monitor. The Moberg CNS monitor is a monitoring device capable of collecting data from multiple devices in high frequency (250 Hz–1000 Hz). The Moberg CNS monitor is connected to the Phillips IntelliVue monitor and to the NIRS-monitor. The system also allows for addition of annotations, i.e., label the data during the clinical procedures in the operating room. The largest advantage, however, is the fact that the Moberg monitor collects all signals with exactly the same timestamp, which is crucial for the analysis of the signals together.

For the microwave links, we use the data collected as part of company's agreements with operators to monitor and improve the operations of the equipment. The data is collected in form of raw signal strength (Tx power, transmit power and Rx, receive power) and the location of the transmitter and receiver. The data is collected in a frequency 1 Hz. The content of the transmitted data is not collected or used in the analysis.

The data is then processed in a similar way. First, we import the data into a Python environment, using the Pandas library. We extract features specific for each domain and then we apply the machine learning algorithms. From the five signals (NIRS, ABP, EEG, ECG, RESP) we extract 48 features in total. From the telecommunication signal strength (Rx), we extract eight features, which characterize the signal – e.g. variation in signal during the minute, standard deviation, mean signal strength. We only use the Rx power as it is the characteristics that is influenced by the disturbance.

In the final stage we use the machine learning anomaly detection and classification algorithms. The results are visualized using the t-SNE diagrams [17] and confusion matrices. We use the standard performance metrics of accuracy, precision, and recall to compare the results. We visualize them using dashboards specific for each of the domains [21, 29].

3.1   Anomaly Detection Algorithms

Anomaly detection is linked to the definition of an anomaly and in our case, we use the definition of an anomaly that is "anomaly is a sudden and short-lived deviation from the normal operation of the network" [1]. The definition has two important components, which are crucial to our study. The first component is the fact that the anomaly is within a network – either a network of telecommunication nodes or a set of signals from the sensors attached to patients. The second component is the fact that the anomaly is short-lived – the duration can differ, but in general it is significantly shorter than the duration of the normal operations.

We can classify algorithms to detect anomalies in data into a number of categories, as proposed by Thudumu et al. [31] or in a wider context by Habeeb et al. [11]:

- Distance-based techniques, where an algorithm measures the distance between a reference data point (e.g., an average) and the current data point; the larger the distance, the more likely the data point is an anomaly.
- Clustering-based techniques, where an algorithm clusters similar data points and identifies the ones that are either in very small clusters or very distant from all existing clusters.
- Density-based techniques, where an algorithm finds data points that are not close to others and therefore can be considered as anomalies.
- Classification-based techniques, where algorithms are trained on example anomalies in order to find similar patterns in the data (which we discuss in Sect. 3.2).

In our work, in order to make the analysis pipeline as similar as possible, and because we use data labelled by specialized physicians, we use Isolation forest as the algorithm [16]. Isolation forest is an ensemble-based classification algorithm, which is based on decision trees, and is therefore analog to Random forest classification algorithm because of that. However, since it is an unsupervised algorithm (does not require labelling), it is similar to clustering algorithms with that respect. The main rationale behind this algorithm is that when a forest of random trees collectively produce shorter path lengths in the decision trees for some particular data points, then these data points are highly likely to be anomalies [16].

An important property of anomaly identification algorithms, including the classification-based techniques like the Isolation forest, is their dependency on the input data. The anomalies are in relation to the input data, which means that when the input data properties change, the algorithm needs to be re-trained. This also means that the smaller the number of data points, the more data points can become anomalies relatively, while the more data points, the anomalies will be fewer. The same dependency is about the variability of the data – the more variability (e.g., in patient signals), the lower number of anomalous data points, as variability is classified as normal data variability, not anomalous.

For the radio link data, we also use a simple threshold technique to automatically identify an anomaly. Since the data is generated by a radio antenna, there should be a minimal variation in the signal strength and therefore all instances of lower signal strength can be considered as anomalies, but without a known source of the anomaly. In other words, this approach allows to quickly identify candidate anomalies, without assigning any classes to it.

3.2 Classification Algorithms

Classification algorithms use the input data to identify patterns and to replicate them on new data. Since they have been used in machine learning almost from the beginning of the existence of the field, there are more than 1,000 such algorithms, excluding the different types of artificial neural networks. There exist event frameworks that allow for automated selection and tuning of the best classification algorithm [8].

By contrast to the anomaly detection algorithms, we label data points explicitly which data points are anomalous and which are not. However, this comes with a cost of annotation and the so-called "imbalanced class problem" [23]. The imbalanced class problem is a problem in which the number of data points in each class is not equal, in particular when one of the classes is much smaller than other classes. This means that the algorithm cannot be trained to distinguish between the classes, as the algorithm can optimize to ignore the imbalanced class without penalty to the performance.

In our study, we chose Random forest [4] algorithm, which is closely related in rationale with the Isolation forest algorithm for anomaly detection. Random forest uses a set of decision trees to train an ensemble of classifiers and use voting strategies to find the best class for a given data point. The algorithm is robust to such aspects as dataset size, balance between classes, number of features and even the number/depth of the decision trees.

4   Data Collection and Analysis Methods

We collect data from two sources, as indicated in Table 1: radio links data (Tx and Rx signals) and patients connected to ICU equipment.

For each **radio link**, we collect the transmission power (Tx) and receive power (Rx) data, which is submitted by the radio network operators. We know the exact location of the link, which allows us to use weather data to annotate an anomaly as related to precipitation or other events.

We define the anomaly in the radio signal as *a sudden and transient loss of signal strength*. An anomaly can be caused by weather phenomena (like precipitation, wind), temporary equipment failure, or obstruction in the signal path (e.g., construction crane).

To annotate this data with weather related anomalies, we use openly available Swedish weather data from the Swedish Weather Authority (SMHI, [30]). The meteorological data contains precipitation observations with up to one minute frequency. The precipitation data contains the amount of precipitation, mm per square meter per minute, and therefore we use a threshold of 0.5 as annotation. If the amount of precipitation is lower than this threshold, we annotate the data point as not-precipitation; if it is higher, we annotate it as precipitation.

In the **ICU**, the following sensors are attached to the patient as the source of data:

- *ECG* (Electro Cardiography), which we use to analyze heart rate variability (HRV). HRV can be defined as a physiological biomarker for the autonomous nervous system and cerebral ischemia has been found to be associated with decreased HRV [27],
- *EEG* (Electroencephalography), which we use to analyze brain activity. EEG is a physiological monitoring technique used to register the brain's electrical activity generated from the cerebral neurons [10],
- *ABP* (Arterial Blood Pressure), which we use to monitor the patient's blood pressure,
- SpO_2 (Blood Oxygen Saturation), which we use to monitor the oxygen saturation in arterial blood, and
- *NIRS* (Near-infrared Spectroscopy), which we use to monitor regional oxygenation in cerebral tissue NIRS is a non-invasive monitoring technique that measures oxygenation in tissues by monitoring light absorption of oxygenated and deoxygenated haemoglobin. NIRS can be used for cerebral oximetry [15].

The signals are recorded by a dedicated equipment, called Moberg monitor (MMM) [6]. MMM provides us with the possibility to record the same time for all signals. In order to process the signals in a uniform way, we need to have the timestamps synchronized. The same timestamp is crucial because we need the synchronized signals for feature extraction. MMM overrides the timestamps of the original sensors and provides the same timestamp for all signals. MMM provides the ability to add the labels to the signals during the data collection. We use that when the physicians add events to the data stream during the operation, for example: start of anaesthesia, clamping of carotid artery, opening of carotid artery, end of anaesthesia and post-operative care.

We defined an anomaly here as *a sudden and transient change of signal caused by the deteriorated cerebral blood flow*. Although such an anomaly can be caused by such conditions as cerebral ischemia, cerebral vasoconstriction, thrombus in cerebral arteries, we collect data from patients undergoing carotid surgery (according to our ethical permission).

Once the data is collected and annotated, we use a t-SNE (t-student distribution Stochastic Network Embedding, [17]) to visualize the multidimensional feature vectors in two dimensional plots. When we apply the anomaly detection or classification algorithms (Isolation forest, Random forest) we measure the accuracy, precision and recall. For the Isolation forest, the accuracy, precision and recall are calculated after the algorithm is applied – first we obtain the classification of a data point to be anomaly (or not) and then we check with the annotated label. For the Random forest, the labels are part of the training of the algorithm (classes) and therefore the algorithm performance metrics are obtained by splitting the data into training and testing datasets (70% vs. 30% respectively).

In addition to the performance measures, we plot confusion matrices to scrutinize quality of the results.

5   Results

For **radio network analysis**, the data that is collected contains two classes – one is the normal operation and then there is the anomalous operation. The t-SNE plot of the data is in Fig. 3. The diagram shows that there are two distinct groups – normal operation points and anomalous points. It shows that these two groups are inherently different, as they form two separate groups. The overlaying value of the classification using the Isolation forest algorithm, however, identifies both anomalous and normal operation points as anomalies. This is shown by the black rectangles being on top of both the normal operation points and anomalous operation points.

The fact that the anomalies are identified with the two groups, and not only in one group, indicates that there is Isolation forest does not consider the precipitation as an anomaly. Isolation forest identifies other variations in the data as anomalies. The confusion matrix is in Fig. 4a for Isolation forest, and it shows that, indeed, the algorithm is unable to identify precipitation as an anomaly.

However, when applying the Random forest algorithm, the confusion matrix, shown in Fig. 4b, shows a different result for the test data. The classification is indeed very accurate and all anomalous data points are identified as anomalies.

For the **ICU**, the visualization of the data points using t-SNE is presented in Fig. 5. The number of classes in the data from ICU is larger and therefore there are more events/classes in the diagram. The results of applying the Isolation forest algorithm to this dataset is visualized by adding the rectangles around the data points classified as anomalous.

The diagram shows that the Isolation forest identifies anomalous data points in a similar way as it does for the radio signal analysis. The anomalous data points belong to all classes, which indicates that the algorithm is not good for the identifying the clamp even (which is anomalous with respect to the other events). For the calculation of accuracy, precision and recall metrics, to make the analysis similar to the radio network analysis, we regard all classes, except for the clamping of artery, as one. Thus we obtain two classes which we can compare to the anomaly analysis (clamping of artery vs. non-clamped artery). When we plot the confusion matrix, Fig. 6a, for the Isolation forest, the results are similar for the radio network analysis.

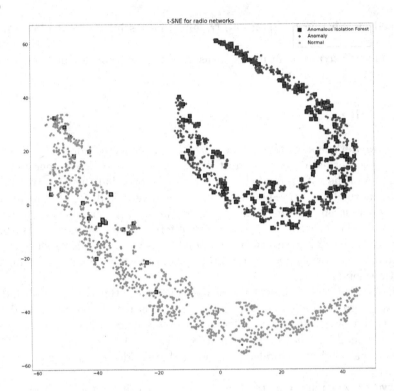

Fig. 3. t-SNE distribution of data points in telecommunication domain.

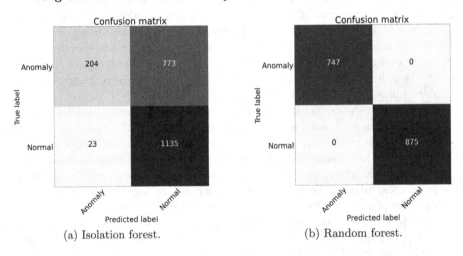

(a) Isolation forest.   (b) Random forest.

Fig. 4. Confusion matrices for the radio network signal classification.

The confusion matrix for two classes is in Fig. 6b for Random forest. In the right-hand side of the figure, we can observe that the results are similar as for

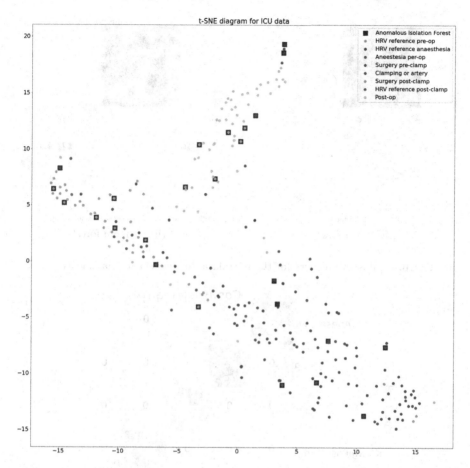

Fig. 5. t-SNE distribution of data points. Colors correspond to events during the carotid surgery. The blue boxes indicate data points identified as anomalous by Isolation forest. (Color figure online)

the telecommunication network signal analysis – Random forest seems to classify the events much better. However, there is one wrongly classified data point – an anomaly classified as a normal operation.

As the data from patients contains more events than normal and anomalous, we can use the Random forest classifier to identify all events (which cannot be done by using Isolation forest, as it only identifies anomalies). The confusion matrix is in Fig. 7 for Random forest. The figure shows that the classification is very accurate and only one data point (row 2) is classified incorrectly as Surgery pre-clamp instead of Clamping of artery.

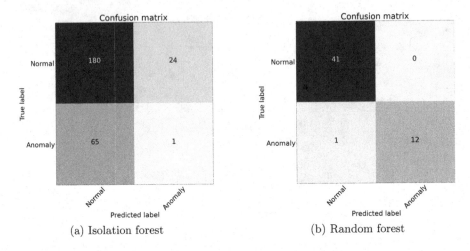

(a) Isolation forest   (b) Random forest

Fig. 6. Confusion matrices for the ICU data, for two classes classification.

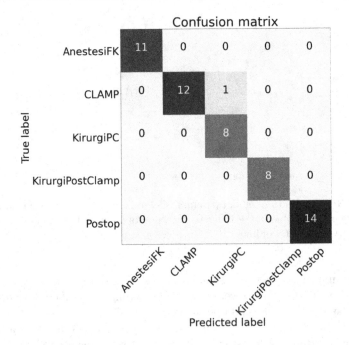

Fig. 7. Confusion matrix for ICU, with multiclass classification.

5.1 Comparison of Algorithms

The performance measures, presented in Fig. 8 show that generally, the performance of the Random forest classifier is higher than the performance of the Isolation forest – for each of the performance metrics.

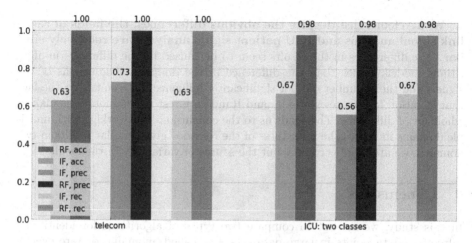

Fig. 8. Performance of machine learning algorithms for both data sets.

Since we only have two classes, the accuracy value of 0.63 for the Isolation forest, shows that the value is close to chance (0.56). Using the Random forest classifier increases the accuracy of the classification of anomalies to 1.0, which is exact. This is also shown in the confusion matrix.

We have also observed that the data from the telecommunication domain, i.e. computer-generated, leads to slightly better results because it is generated. There are no incorrect classifications when using the Random forest algorithm. This can be caused by the fact that the ICU data can contain noise introduced during the clinical procedures or during the annotation of the data. It can also show that there is a natural degree of similarity between different events as the patient-generated data has natural variability (e.g., all hearts beat slightly different).

5.2   Lesson's Learned

In addition to the evaluation of the algorithms in this setting, we have also found a number of important facts from the study.

First, we observed that **the definition of what an anomaly is gives more benefit than the algorithm used to identify it.** Although finding anomalies is important, it is often a proxy for finding *specific* kinds of anomalies. Even in the domain of radio signal analysis, the most important part is to know what the anomaly is (or what it could be caused by) in order to find a proper action plan to either prevent such anomalies or reduce their effects. Statistical anomalies are of less interest as they can be caused by unknown, and therefore irrelevant, factors.

Therefore, we found that it is better to discuss *rare events* rather than anomalies. Rare events can be described and classified, whereas anomalies can remain to be undefined and unknown. This helps to select the right algorithms.

We also found that **despite the obvious differences, the fields of radio link signal analysis and ICU patient signal analyses are relatively similar.** The differences in the results seem to be caused by the difference in algorithms/models rather than the difference in the domains. The origins of the signals and their number did not significantly influence the results, but the fact that Isolation forest uses statistics and Random forest uses annotations make a whole lot of difference. This leads us to the conclusion that working with multiple domains increases the robustness of the results – given similar results in two domains, we are more certain about the source of variability in the results.

6   Conclusions

In this study, we set out to compare two types of algorithms for identifying infrequent data points in large data sets – so called anomalies or rare events. These infrequent data points are of importance as they can indicate abnormal operation of equipment, e.g., in the telecommunication radio network analysis, or certain clinical conditions, e.g., the cerebral ischemia in stroke patients.

We compared Random forest and Isolation forest algorithms, which are conceptually very similar, despite targeting different classes of problems – classification of data (Random forest) vs. anomaly identification (Isolation forest). The results show that the classification algorithm outperforms the anomaly analysis algorithms – 100% accuracy compared to 73% accuracy. We have also found that the initial effort put into annotation of the data leads to more actionable results. The algorithms provide the information what kind of anomaly it is and therefore the user can take the appropriate action.

In our further work, we intend to expand the study to compare data from more domains and complement these algorithms with the AutoML approach to find the optimal algorithm for the data from each domain.

References

1. Ahmed, T., Oreshkin, B., Coates, M.: Machine learning approaches to network anomaly detection. In: Proceedings of the 2nd USENIX Workshop on Tackling Computer Systems Problems with Machine Learning Techniques, pp. 1–6. USENIX Association (2007)
2. Alghushairy, O., Alsini, R., Soule, T., Ma, X.: A review of local outlier factor algorithms for outlier detection in big data streams. Big Data Cogn. Comput. **5**(1), 1 (2020)
3. Block, L., El-Merhi, A., Liljencrantz, J., Naredi, S., Staron, M., Odenstedt Hergès, H.: Cerebral ischemia detection using artificial intelligence (CIDAI) - a study protocol. Acta Anaesthesiol. Scand. **64**(9), 1335–1342 (2020)
4. Breiman, L.: Random forests. Mach. Learn. **45**(1), 5–32 (2001)
5. Chwala, C., Kunstmann, H.: Commercial microwave link networks for rainfall observation: assessment of the current status and future challenges. Wiley Interdiscip. Rev. Water **6**(2), e1337 (2019)

6. Citerio, G., et al.: Data collection and interpretation. Neurocrit. Care **22**(3), 360–368 (2015)
7. Eltanbouly, S., Bashendy, M., AlNaimi, N., Chkirbene, Z., Erbad, A.: Machine learning techniques for network anomaly detection: a survey. In: 2020 IEEE International Conference on Informatics, IoT, and Enabling Technologies (ICIoT), pp. 156–162. IEEE (2020)
8. Feurer, M., Eggensperger, K., Falkner, S., Lindauer, M., Hutter, F.: Auto-sklearn 2.0: hands-free AutoML via meta-learning. arXiv preprint arXiv:2007.04074 (2020)
9. Gao, Y., Ao, H., Wang, K., Zhou, W., Li, Y.: The diagnosis of wired network malfunctions based on big data and traffic prediction: an overview. In: 2015 4th International Conference on Computer Science and Network Technology (ICCSNT), vol. 1, pp. 1204–1208. IEEE (2015)
10. Gaspard, N.: Current clinical evidence supporting the use of continuous EEG monitoring for delayed cerebral ischemia detection. J. Clin. Neurophysiol. **33**(3), 211–216 (2016)
11. Habeeb, R.A.A., Nasaruddin, F., Gani, A., Hashem, I.A.T., Ahmed, E., Imran, M.: Real-time big data processing for anomaly detection: a survey. Int. J. Inf. Manage. **45**, 289–307 (2019)
12. Haixiang, G., Yijing, L., Shang, J., Mingyun, G., Yuanyue, H., Bing, G.: Learning from class-imbalanced data: review of methods and applications. Expert Syst. Appl. **73**, 220–239 (2017)
13. Hubert, M., Debruyne, M., Rousseeuw, P.J.: Minimum covariance determinant and extensions. Wiley Interdiscip. Rev. Comput. Stat. **10**(3), e1421 (2018)
14. Komorowski, M.: Artificial intelligence in intensive care: are we there yet? Intensive Care Med. **45**(9), 1298–1300 (2019). https://doi.org/10.1007/s00134-019-05662-6
15. Lewis, C., Parulkar, S.D., Bebawy, J., Sherwani, S., Hogue, C.W.: Cerebral neuromonitoring during cardiac surgery: a critical appraisal with an emphasis on near-infrared spectroscopy. J. Cardiothorac. Vasc. Anesth. **32**(5), 2313–2322 (2018)
16. Liu, F.T., Ting, K.M., Zhou, Z.H.: Isolation forest. In: 2008 Eighth IEEE International Conference on Data Mining, pp. 413–422. IEEE (2008)
17. Maaten, L.V.D., Hinton, G.: Visualizing data using t-SNE. J. Mach. Learn. Res. **9**(11), 2579–2605 (2008)
18. Maringer, E.F., Shiland, J., Brodie, D.: There's more to medicine than machines. Intensive Care Med. **44**(6), 930–931 (2018)
19. Musumeci, F., et al.: Supervised and semi-supervised learning for failure identification in microwave networks. IEEE Trans. Netw. Serv. Manage. **18**(2), 1934–1945 (2020)
20. Omar, S., Ngadi, A., Jebur, H.H.: Machine learning techniques for anomaly detection: an overview. Int. J. Comput. Appl. **79**(2) (2013)
21. Pandazo, K., Shollo, A., Staron, M., Meding, W.: Presenting software metrics indicators: a case study. In: Proceedings of the 20th International Conference on Software Product and Process Measurement (MENSURA), vol. 20 (2010)
22. Polz, J., Chwala, C., Graf, M., Kunstmann, H.: Rain event detection in commercial microwave link attenuation data using convolutional neural networks. Atmos. Meas. Tech. **13**(7), 3835–3853 (2020)
23. Provost, F.: Machine learning from imbalanced data sets 101. In: Proceedings of the AAAI'2000 Workshop on Imbalanced Data Sets, vol. 68, pp. 1–3. AAAI Press (2000)
24. Pudashine, J., et al.: Deep learning for an improved prediction of rainfall retrievals from commercial microwave links. Water Resour. Res. **56**(7) (2020)

25. Ramos, L.A., et al.: Machine learning improves prediction of delayed cerebral ischemia in patients with subarachnoid hemorrhage. J. Neurointerv. Surg. **11**(5), 497–502 (2019)

26. Sandberg, A., Pareto, L., Arts, T.: Agile collaborative research: action principles for industry-academia collaboration. IEEE Softw. **28**(4), 74–83 (2011)

27. Schmidt, J.M.: Heart rate variability for the early detection of delayed cerebral ischemia. J. Clin. Neurophysiol. **33**(3), 268–274 (2016)

28. Staron, M., et al.: Robust machine learning in critical care - software engineering and medical perspectives. In: 2021 IEEE/ACM 1st Workshop on AI Engineering-Software Engineering for AI (WAIN), pp. 62–69. IEEE (2021)

29. Staron, M., Meding, W., Caiman, M.: Improving completeness of measurement systems for monitoring software development workflows. In: Winkler, D., Biffl, S., Bergsmann, J. (eds.) SWQD 2013. LNBIP, vol. 133, pp. 230–243. Springer, Heidelberg (2013). https://doi.org/10.1007/978-3-642-35702-2_14

30. Swedish Meteorological Institute: SMHI öppna data meteorologiska observationer (2017). https://www.smhi.se

31. Thudumu, S., Branch, P., Jin, J., Singh, J.J.: A comprehensive survey of anomaly detection techniques for high dimensional big data. J. Big Data **7**(1), 1–30 (2020). https://doi.org/10.1186/s40537-020-00320-x

Author Index

A
Alégroth, Emil 17
Ali, Nauman Bin 87
Atzberger, Daniel 41

B
Block, Linda 121
Börstler, Jürgen 87

C
Cech, Tim 41

D
Döllner, Jürgen 41

G
Gonzalez-Huerta, Javier 17
Gordieieva, Daria 109
Gordieiev, Oleksandr 109

H
Hergés, Helena Odenstedt 121

I
Iftikhar, Umar 87

L
Lind, Emil 17

M
Misra, Sanjay 41

P
Plösch, Reinhold 63

R
Rainer, Austen 109
Ramler, Rudolf 63

S
Scheibel, Willy 41
Sjödin, Martin 121
Smite, Darja 3
Stadler, Philipp 63
Staron, Miroslaw 121

U
Usman, Muhammad 87

© The Editor(s) (if applicable) and The Author(s), under exclusive license
to Springer Nature Switzerland AG 2023
D. Mendez et al. (Eds.): SWQD 2023, LNBIP 472, p. 137, 2023.
https://doi.org/10.1007/978-3-031-31488-9

Printed in the United States
by Baker & Taylor Publisher Services